Dear A

"THE CHOICE"

(from footlights to faith)

Blessings - and very best wishes

BETH ELLIS

Beth Ellis

BETHELLIS BOOKS

STOKE GOLDING
✠
BETHELLIS
BOOKS

ISBN: 978-1-910181-23-2

Printed and Published by
AnchorPrint Group Ltd

In association with:
BETHELLIS BOOKS
Stoke Golding,
England
Email: bethellisdreams@gmail.com

Cover Design by Josh Diboll

Loving Acknowledgements

This journey of exploration, learning about a young Carpenter from Nazareth, has taken me half way round the world. I know that I've met Him through all of you.

Jenny Jones who self published her own book, unwittingly became the catalyst for me to publish mine. Her advice has been invaluable. Also, this year my long-time friend Eileen Jackson urged me to dig *my* book out again. She ordered me back to my computer, saying 'this is the year we're going to see it published'. Without the determination of Eileen, and her patient encouragement, as she worked with me on every chapter telling me 'we're nearly there Beth', this book would not have seen the light of day. I can never thank her enough. (if we're still friends)!

Sally Raynham and Elizabeth Williams have undertaken the meticulous proof-reading, both in their spare time, a superb job well done.

Bernadette Meyers, a gifted photographer has generously given me her time and expertise designing the complete layout of the photos, and deserves an enormous thank you from me.

To the many dedicated teacher, leaders and pastors of Youth With a Mission in the UK and in the other nations I visited, who patiently taught me by example. Thank you that you constantly forgave the foibles of this actress who wanted to play the part of a Missionary

But it's to Bruce - Rev Bruce Collins, Adam's faithful friend and prayer partner, who gave me his care and support when I most needed it at Adam's murder, that I dedicate this book. He unknowingly gave me the idea for the title, as he prayed with me, gently urging me to make 'The Choice', pointing the way. Bruce and the many members of St Peter's Church, Notting Hill Gate rallied round us through two traumatic losses, and were our first church 'family'.

My love goes to my two beautiful granddaughters Charlotte and Katy and their busy violinist Mum – Rachel, - my *Ruth.*

Joshua Diboll, aspiring student journalist, designed the cover for me and put up with his grandmother's constant emails niggling over tiny details. Thanks Josh.

Finally to my darling daughter Amanda, who has put up with me talking about this project for the last twenty years. It is finished sweetheart. Love Mum.

Contents

ACT ONE

ACT TWO

ACT THREE

EPILOGUE

ACT ONE

PROLOGUE: AUGUST 25TH 1988

"West London Police are trying to identify the body of a young man found lying on the towpath of the Grand Union Canal, stabbed to death apparently while fishing. Will anyone with any information please ring 999."

That short statement on the BBC six o'clock news in August 1988 changes my life forever.

1

MURDER AND ITS CONSEQUENCES

Notting Hill is enjoying an August heat wave. Tomorrow Carnival begins: our Caribbean Street party. People either love it or loathe it. After all the years I've lived here I still love it. Leaving the window wide open, I curl up on the sofa lazily watching the six o'clock news. The phone rings. I hear the worried voice of my son's girlfriend: "Beth, did Adam stay with you last night?"

"No Scina, why?"

"I left him fishing at the canal around nine yesterday, and we arranged to go to the Proms tonight, but his flat mates say he hasn't been home."

"Well he hasn't been here." Seriously puzzled I continue making stupid suggestions. "Have you been back to the Canal where you left him? See if any of his fishing tackle's there, or... or..." I stop, hearing a sentence on the television:

"*West London police are trying to identify the body of a young man found lying on the towpath of the Grand Union Canal, stabbed to death apparently while fishing. Will anyone with any information please ring 999.*"

"Scina, I need to ring 999. I'll be in touch as soon as I know what's happening." This can't be Adam. Things like this don't happen to people like me.

"Oh 999? – I've just heard your announcement, and my son is missing, and..." I wait .... At last they arrive, two of them. They glance at me apologetically and ask, "Have you a photograph?" I find one, with Adam sitting on a fence in summer sunshine with his sister Amanda. They show me a watch in a plastic envelope, "Do you recognise this watch?"

"It's the one I gave him for his last birthday."

"*I'm sorry Mrs Ellis, it **is** your son.*"

Adam was found stabbed through the heart. Lying on the towpath – alone. Happy fishing when Scina left him.... Oh yes! Scina will be waiting.

The policewoman goes to break the news to her. Now, what must I do? Who must I tell? Where can I start? With close friends Diana and Jim.

"We'll be right over."

Now Adam's father, Jimmy (my ex). His wife answers, and gasps, "Murder... Oh no. Jimmy's at Lord's for the cricket, I'll try to trace him."

Next, I ring my brother in Cheshire. His wife Anne replies, "No - Oh no."

Wearily I assure her, 'Yes Anne, Yes."

Now Amanda; how can I tell her that her adored brother has been murdered? In the Surrey countryside, their phone keeps ringing. They'll be at the pub. It's Friday evening and Bank Holiday. I find my son Hugo's new number in Brighton. Again there's no answer. I ring another actress friend who lives there and tell her the news. 'Leave it to me Beth, I'll find him."

While I'm waiting, the large photograph of Ibsen's "Ghosts" on the wall catches my attention. In desperation Mrs Alving leans over her son as he is dying. I remember how the director made me bring the play to its tragic end with a heartbreaking wail of woe, and here I am with this policeman calmly talking about the stabbing of my firstborn son.

People start arriving, Jim and Diana first. Their daughter Jane has been given the task of finding Amanda and telling her to drive straight to London. Jimmy arrives with his friend from Lords, looking confused and uncomprehending, asking the same questions all over again.

Amanda comes running in, in floods of tears: rushing to comfort me, and to be comforted. Diana announces that I'm not to stay here. We're all to stay with her and Jim in Twickenham.

"Go and pack a few things."

"Yes but I still need to find Hugo." Diana has arranged all that. He's been found. Daughter Jane and her husband are driving them to Twickenham. I submit to everyone's plans for me, allowing myself to be bundled into a car, along with Florence, our collie. She knows something bad is happening in all our lives. Cowed and shivering she nestles close to me for comfort.

We huddle together in Diana's front room, talking disjointedly. Nothing's real any more. A car engine revs outside and stops. Doors slam shut. Hugo, lanky-framed, six foot four, just seventeen months younger than his brother, stands stock-still in the front garden.

He's in tears, unable to move. Amanda runs out, throwing her arms around him. I follow. We cling to each other for protection from this nightmare, perhaps hoping our physical closeness will somehow make it go away.

"We've got each other. We must hang on in there, close together."

Someone else is standing In the light of the porch. Jimmy: undecided whether he should join us. 'We need you Jimmy." The four of us hold on to each other.

By now it's 1.00 am. Time to go to bed. Since 6.00 pm our lives have been changed forever. Adam has been violently murdered. He won't start his new course on Tuesday after Bank Holiday. I don't want to go to bed: I'm too frightened. It feels too dangerous being alone. I long for Jimmy to stay with us. Adam was *our* son, not just mine. But his wife and child are also worrying and waiting for him. So Amanda stays close, reaching out her hand, on a mattress next to my bed.
Diana gives me a pill and sleep takes over: dark and dreamless.

Waking early next morning, gradually

everything begins flooding back. A moan, a sound of pain. Deep down somewhere, the sound surfaces, the saddest, wounded groan. Where is it coming from? Rising involuntarily from the deepest part of me. No Beth, this isn't a nightmare. It's horribly real. There's no more Adam - he's gone. Yesterday he was alive. Now I no longer have him. Tears start, choking, helpless sobbing. Amanda's arms are around me, comforting me. The next two days, we all just huddle together. Diana, somehow, is constantly providing meals. Sitting around their kitchen table we talk about what we need to do next.

Finally the time comes. We have to begin again. The Bank Holiday is over. The Caribbean carnival-goers have gone home. I shall also go home, on my own, and pick up the pieces....

The police have a suspect: Christopher, a young Irishman from Cork. He was seen on the towpath, and when passers-by saw Adam fall they rang the police. The following morning at dawn, there is a knock at his door, and he is arrested.

Adam's body can only be released from the morgue once his father and Jim Greene identify him after the Bank Holiday. Then the official machinery starts humming into place.

The funeral. Which church? We decide it should be at St John's in Ladbroke Grove, where Adam and Hugo carried the candles years ago as little boys, and where they were both baptised when the Nanny we had at the time insisted on their 'religious instruction'.

The young curate of St Peter's, twinned with St John's; our local parish church speaks to the whole family about the service. Bruce Collins has been a constant friend to Adam, and I ring him immediately after that first police visit. I know I can count on his wisdom, his advice and his constant support. Knowing nothing about church services we leave it mainly to Bruce.

"Do you have a Bible?"

I begin looking along the shelves for the little green Sunday School Bible I'd been given as a child, and then admit: "I'm sorry Bruce, I don't think we do." The one thing I am passionate about is being allowed to speak about my Adam at this last official function for him. Bruce firmly assures me, "This is your family funeral Beth; you can do what you want for Adam."

Jimmy had been in a BBC television favourite "Z Cars", so mountains of letters keep arriving, many from television colleagues. The most moving though are from Adam's few friends, and I'm determined to read them out. Once I say I want to speak, Jimmy decides that he'd like to read a poem by John Donne. Hugo reads from Hamlet, and Amanda writes a poem of memories as a final goodbye to her brother, which she asks Diana to read for her.

To Adam – with love from Mandy

Oh! Adam – first born son
of Beth and James,
your journey's done.

You've stepped beyond
the world's embrace
and heaven's welcome rim
you trace.

But Adam,
could you wait before
you step through
God's immortal door.

For these few words
I'd like to say
for you to take
along your way....

Thank you for all
the fun you brought,
our childhood games
and battles fought.

The struggles and
the tears as well,
the three of us
inseparable.

But mostly, I would
thank you for
that part of you
which I adored.

Your gentleness,
your simple faith
in goodness
and the human race.

*Your pure ability
to love –
you haven't taken
that above.*

*You've left it here
within my heart
as memories,
a constant part*

*Of you, I'll carry
'til the date
that we're rejoined
at heaven's gate.*

Eddie, a gentle Scotsman and one of the lads who have shared the house with Adam, plucks up the courage to say a few words as well.

Our next duty is to say goodbye to Adam at the funeral parlour. Apart from my Mother I've never seen anyone lying in a coffin, and I certainly never expected to see my son in one. Going in as a family, the undertaker gently suggests that we might all have 'a wee drink'. Is it really true that we can't experience pain without alcohol?

"You'll find it easier to handle seeing your loved one. We've done our best to cover up the bruises on his face."

Everyone grabs the glass of brandy offered. To my amazement I find myself saying, "No thanks, I don't drink." After just six weeks of A.A. meetings, this is a small miracle. I examine Adam's face closely. His expression is somehow disapproving, even severe. I know the undertakers have tried to cover up the grazing and bruises from the attack, but I can see them. I feel so angry that anyone should violate Adam, my gentle Christian son. Why did he have to die so brutally, so fearfully, and especially, so alone? I long to have been there to protect him. Adam has always been so vulnerable. We've been struggling together for years to find the right medication, to get that complete stability in his life. Finally, it seems we have. He's been accepted to start a new training: framing pictures with some artist friends. Scina has also been such a support to him. She's a shy Italian woman, a few years older than Adam, and sharing the same love of classical music. I think he was very much in love with her. I sense loneliness and loss, and again that question. Why?

Warm September sunshine, brilliant in an endless blue sky, greets the day of the funeral. Sitting outside the church in our official family limousine, watching everyone arriving, Hugo whispers, "Mummy, the whole of our lives are out there." I imagine he is recognizing all those actor friends he has seen as a little boy, coming to our home in Holland Park; constant guests of Jimmy's and mine. At last we make that long walk in and take our seats at the front of the packed church. Bruce is standing at the altar steps waiting for Adam's coffin.

Jimmy has insisted that, in the Irish tradition, his son will be carried by the men of the family rather than by professional pallbearers. They stride down the centre of the church with Adam lifted high. Seeing Jimmy carrying his son in such a tragic circumstance has an extraordinary effect on the congregation: people weep, setting the tone for the entire service. The whole family is sharing openly and personally. Eddie, the

Scotsman from Adam's shared house is a joy. His description of his first meeting with Adam, when he was suffering from an attack of deep depression, is so funny and typical of Adam: trying to cheer someone up when he felt they needed encouraging. It's a comforting light note, allowing everyone to laugh.

We end the service with the wonderful theme music from the film The Mission. This was a favourite of Adam's. His flat mates confirm that they would always groan, "Oh no Adam – not The Mission again!" Now these haunting Amazon Indian pipes are redolent of everything about Adam and his violent death. The Mission shows the appalling slaughter of innocent young American Indians in the name of Religion. Adam's natural compassion has always been open and available. It's as if Adam is speaking through that music as it fills the church.

I hug each person as they come out into the brilliant September sunshine, separately thanking each one and wanting them to know how much their coming has meant to us all. Now it's time for us to follow Adam to the crematorium.

The Kensal Rise cemetery and the crematorium service are full of gentleness and it comforts me. The cemetery is not a sad place, even though it flanks the bank of the canal where Adam fell and died. There is stillness and peace in the midst of London's hectic bustling activity, and the short service led by Bruce is a form of closure.

The key to my home is with a friend, and an amazing team has taken over making plates of sandwiches, every kind of homemade pastry and pots of tea and coffee. I'll always remember the very beautiful golden/green teapot which my actor friend Paul gives me. It belonged to his mother from Austria and is much larger than mine. I keep it for years until a crack in the base means it has to go.

Arriving home I find an atmosphere of genuine affection. People are in the garden or on the terrace in the sunshine, looking after each other. Bruce is with us, making easy conversation with everyone. I have never hosted anything at home that I have not personally organised and controlled meticulously, but today everyone else takes over. Surprisingly I find it the most beautiful day. Towards the end someone remarks to me as they are leaving, "Beth this has been the saddest day for you, but think what it must be like for Christopher's mother."

"Yes I know Maggie, I've often thought of her already. I've thought of the knock on her door, and being told the news. My heart goes out to her." We hug. I let her go. It's all over. I'm on my own.

The flat's emptiness scares me and echoes my own fear. Everything in life seems vulnerable, precarious. I'm not sure what to do. Everyone has been so kind. Cups and saucers are washed up and put away. There's nothing left for me to do.

I plump up a few cushions on the sofa, and find myself staring at the framed sepia photographs of my parents, my baby brother, and me back in the 1920s and 30s.

" the large photograph of Ibsen's Ghosts with Hugo catches my attention." p.9.

The three of us inseparable.

Adam at my sixtieth birthday,
a month before his murder.

I found a photograph of Adam in a sunny field with his sister Amanda.

My very beautiful mother with her
Marcel wave.

Daddy aged 24 in his new tropical 'whites'.

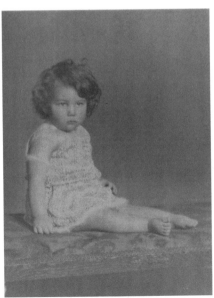

A very solemn moment -
where are my shoes?

Mummy escaping 'upcountry' in her topee
and shorts.

Never a promising ballerina.

Singapore Christmas present with
baby brother Stuart

Singapore - Stuart and I with our
much loved Ayah

Port Said on one of our many sailings
from Singapore to the UK.

2

SINGAPORE - 'PORT OF THE LION': 1928

That small island at the tip of the peninsula of what was then called The Federated Malay States. That's where it all begins. My father is one of that enthusiastic band of young men from the UK who are drawn to the opportunities awaiting them in the British Colonies just after the Great War. Vast numbers went to East Africa, India and, of course, the Far East. My father is just twenty-four when he marries my mother, and is then given the chance to join the Singapore branch of the British firm he is working for, allied to the Borneo Trading Company. I believe he starts out as some sort of travelling salesman. This means long pioneering journeys into the interior – up country. In those early days this involves tediously slow train journeys and then staying with local employees of the company in their bungalows, rather than in smart modern hotels. My mother quite often accompanies him rather than being left behind, not knowing a soul, and having to deal with the terrifyingly snobbish Singapore social set. At twenty-two, from a working class background, she finds the transition to being a 'Mem' in charge of a household with two Chinese servants, fairly traumatic. So she escapes, wearing her topee and khaki shorts (she is a very pretty woman) into places in the interior of the Malay Peninsula and Borneo where none of the British mems would dream of going. I arrive a couple of years later in 1928. By this time my parents have become accustomed to the British Colonial life-style, and having made their own circle of friends, are happily living a very privileged existence.

From the time my memory starts to function, life seems to be a round of weekend parties at the Swimming Club and Changi Beach; my mother's Mah Jong parties in the morning; tennis parties in the afternoon, and dinner parties in the evenings. After my younger brother and I have been bathed and pyjama'd by Ayah, we are taken into the guests, all in their evening dress, to kiss everyone goodnight. My mother then comes in to hear our prayers, "Gentle Jesus meek and mild look upon a little child..." It is all very J M Barrie and the Darling family from Peter Pan. We even have a large dog as a guardian: an Alsatian called Jane. She is the sweetest, most loving animal that my father has rescued from the RSPCA.

After we are tucked in behind our mosquito nets, I crawl out and lie on the floor, to watch those lovely glittery people I can see so easily below the saloon-style swing doors. Daddy, in his immaculate white sharkskin jacket and evening dress trousers. Mummy and the ladies in those glamorous backless gowns of the thirties, cut on the cross, clinging to their figures. The big overhead fan whirrs softly in the ceiling, while Ah Chin and Ah Lak are serving trays of drinks. Martinis, Gin and Tonics, Pink Gins, and Whisky Sodas. At nine years old I already love the glamour of party-time and dressing up. One night I am eventually discovered, having fallen asleep on the floor. My mother trips over me in the dark as she brings some of the ladies through to our bathroom. I am gently teased about it next morning. Ours is an idyllic childhood, full of sunshine and swimming, and happy schooldays with so many friends. We are materially spoilt, with everything done for us. We beg the servants to let us learn to clean our shoes as a special treat.

On the other hand, my father is fairly frightening. He is a great one for authority and discipline, and reduces me to tears in his efforts to help me with my arithmetic homework. I soon learn never to ask for his help, and to suffer bad marks rather than have his six foot three inch frame lowering over me, his eyes spitting anger at my total ignorance, his voice rising in exasperation at my inability to answer his questions, while tears plop onto my sandaled feet. At all other times he is my hero. As well as being the undisputed head of our family, he is also the Commissioner of Scouts for Singapore, and brings me up to be a Baden-Powell girl. He is also a disciple of Kipling, and I am taught IF by the age of seven. "If you can keep your head when all about you are losing theirs and blaming it on you... If – If –If...You'll be a man my son!" The fact that I am his daughter never seems to register with either of us.

He always attends all the official Colonial military parades held before breakfast in the cool of the morning, at the Singapore *Padang*. The Singapore Cricket Pavilion is in the middle distance, while St Andrews, the Anglican Cathedral where I've been exquisitely baptised with all the trimmings, forms the background. I'll always remember those misty early mornings wearing my pith helmet against the forthcoming sun, clutching my father's hand, and watching the soldiers in gleaming white and scarlet. Their helmets are dramatically topped with silver spikes and feathery plumes. The men march up and down in intricate formations amongst the gleaming brass instruments of the military bands. There is always a great rolling of drums, ending with God Save the King. Every person on that parade ground is at stiff attention!

I am mortified when my father taps the shoulder of an elderly Chinaman standing in front of us, demanding he should remove his hat immediately out of respect to our King during the Anthem.

My early upbringing is very much Honour and Glory to King and Country and the Great British Empire. Currently all very Politically Incorrect.

Inevitably, the time comes when we have to be sent to our big schools in England. In the 1930s the normal practice is for all UK children to go to boarding school at the age of nine or ten, after attending Tanglin Preparatory School. As far as I know this was the only all-white school in Singapore in those sad race-prejudiced days. My brother Stuart is two and a half years younger than I am, and neither of us has known any way of life, other than our charmed existence in 17 Orange Grove Road with Muna, our Malay ayah, who is married to Kubun, our gardener. They live in their small flat of two rooms over the garage at the end of the drive. They are Moslem, and not long before we leave Singapore, we lose our gentle Muna, as she is childless. Kubun, by Moslem law, divorces her, and she is sent back to her family in Java (now Indonesia). She and I often spend afternoons sitting on the nursery steps talking in Malay to each other, while she combs and oils her waist length hair in the sun. It is black and glossy like a raven's wing. I dearly love her. Her leaving us is my first remembered experience of loss.

Our two Chinese houseboys are subjected to merciless teasing by Stuart and me. We go to their servants' quarters at the back of the house, and lift each other up to peer through a high peephole to catch them naked in the shower. They never seem to be angry with us, just chasing us away, laughing and waving their arms in mock threats.

We have so many special parties with

loads of people in our compound, which is next to the Borneo Company's bachelor bungalow. About four of the company's young bachelors, straight out from the UK, are housed there, so anytime we are having a special do they are invited over as a matter of course. The bonfire party with fireworks and sparklers on Guy Fawkes Day, for instance, is always a splendid affair for both adults and children alike. We children are all dressed up in our best party clothes. Today we would be in tee shirts and jeans, but then I am in a brand new white multi-frilled organza party dress. Suddenly, one of the sparks from my hand-held sparkler sets my dress on fire. The frills become instant flames and I am immediately wrapped in an adult's coat and rolled on the ground in it. Fortunately, Auntie Nell, my father's secretary, has the presence of mind to grab me like that. Sadly, it is the end of my pretty new party frock, but apart from the shock, I am completely unharmed.

Auntie Nell – Helen (Nell) McBride - is one of our closest family friends, and she is married to Uncle Norman, who is a number of years older than her. He is head of one of the departments of Robinson's; Singapore's very traditional and much-loved Department Store, in the same main square as my father's office. Nell is his secretary and Auntie to my brother and me. One day I ask Mummy why we never ask her to come to the Swimming Club with us. Her explanation is made in the same confidential tone that parents adopt when trying to discuss difficult subjects like *where do babies come from?*

"Well you see darling, Auntie Nell is Eurasian, and isn't allowed to be a member of the Swimming Club."

"What is Eurasian Mummy?"

"It means that one of her parents isn't white."

"But she looks white."

"Yes I know, some people do, but you can tell by the texture of the skin, it's not as smooth as ours. And then there's the way they speak, with a different intonation."

I suppose I am seven or eight, and Nell is the only person who has the presence of mind to wrap me in her coat when my party frock leaps into flames. It is very muddling for me.

My mother doesn't tell me not to mention our conversation to Nell, so I don't realise that it's a secret. I see her at the Swimming Club one day as the guest of someone who presumably hasn't been told this terrible fact, and I ask her how she's been allowed in. There are red faces all round. One day, Nell tells me that her father was a Scotsman in the Merchant Navy, and while his ship had been in port in Singapore, he had fallen in love with a beautiful Malayan girl, and Nell is the daughter of their marriage. It is also the reason that she and Uncle Norman have decided not to have any children: in case the colour of their skin will prove without doubt that there is *a touch of the tar brush* – an expression sometimes used in those days.

Another vivid memory of the mysterious black and white rules of those days is when Mummy and I are on a shopping expedition in the City centre. We were probably going to Robinson's. Mummy parks the car in the square, where there is a Tamil car park attendant. Mummy marches off ahead of me, looking impeccably elegant as always. I start to run after her, when the attendant sees a car approaching and puts his hand on my shoulder to stop me. My mother turns round at that moment and, seeing his hand on my shoulder, orders him to remove it immediately. I run over to her explaining, "Mummy, Mummy, he stopped me from being run over." and insist she must say thank–you. It is all so confusing. We are entrusted to Ayah and Kubun, and to Ah Chin and Ah Lak whenever my parents go away, but any other black, brown or non-white person is suspect. I'm sure my parents aren't unkind or particularly prejudiced people. They look after our domestic staff with care and affection as part of the family. Sadly, those seemed to be the rules in our great British Colonies in the thirties. Only the very enlightened liberal would consider questioning them.

One of the most painful things about leaving Singapore is having to say goodbye to all our school friends; to our adored Alsatian Jane, and for me, secretly, my rocking horse. Perhaps nearing ten years old is too old to still be in love with one's toys, but he is real to me. I talk to him as we rock back and forth, my arms round his neck, my cheek on the grey hair of his mane, telling him my thoughts in his ear. He is too big to be included in our packing cases though, and I suppose Mummy thinks I will soon outgrow him. So he has to be hugged and kissed and given away. More loss.

On the other hand, there is the excitement of going to England and seeing snow and ice. I have to wear a liberty bodice, with long black school stockings. The liberty bodice is an extraordinary garment. Like a vest, but with little rubber buttons at the bottom to attach suspenders for those long black lisle school stockings. They all make me feel so grown up, although I have no idea why they are called liberty bodices. My navy blue school gymslip and crisp white blouse, along with a bottle green blazer and matching gloves are packed away at the bottom of the linen chest, brought back from our last leave in the UK. Our lives are always split up into three years out East, and then six months' leave in the UK – as if we are in the Services.

Apart from the packing cases, which are stowed away in the holds, there are those wonderfully nostalgic cabin trunks. With their shiny brass studs all round the outside edges, they open up to reveal a miniature hanging wardrobe on one side, and three deep drawers on the other. I keep one for many years. It is invaluable for my first years in the theatre, going away into rep for extended seasons of anything up to a year. In these days, however, without the luxury of porters, sadly they are redundant. I wish I still had it though, with all those romantic labels – P & O LINE – BLUE FUNNEL LINE – SINGAPORE – MARSEILLES – TILBURY; so redolent of the elegance of travel in those pre-war days.

My memory of that last sailing from Singapore is still vivid, as I move away from the rest of the family group to be on my own. I watch the docks and warehouses, the shoreline of that island slipping away. It's dusk, and the ship's funnels are booming their farewell into the gathering evening. Leaning on the rail, I whisper my goodbyes into the wind: to Singapore and its people where I've been so happy and knew I belonged. I promise 'I will come back one day, I promise never to forget you.' As every child knows, if you promise something, nothing will prevent you from fulfilling that promise.

The image, still so strong, of that small figure standing alone, whispering into the wind, and in tears at the sense of even more loss, makes me wonder if in some subliminal way, I am also saying goodbye to my childhood, and to the end of an era. I am nearly ten, and in six months' time I will be going to my Big School as a boarder, in somewhere called Cuckfield, Sussex. Mummy and Daddy will have to leave us in England, and we will probably only see them once a year for the next three years. It is a new episode in our lives. Singapore and our blissful existence is coming to an end. We can't hang on to it any longer. This is 1938. Change is coming, not only for the little girl in that image, but also for the whole of Singapore and The Federated Malay States, and especially for the very place we are heading; Great Britain and the entire Continent of Europe. Am I sensing some sort of prophetic foreboding of the future, even at nine and a half?

Marseilles. It is always our last port of call, and we know that we are now truly in Europe. My mother always takes us shopping for the last few items of clothing we are going to need in England. Buying a pair of rather beautiful leather gloves, for best is an adventure I always remember with great delight. I am perched on a high stool by the glass glove counter, and then shown how to lean my hand and arm onto a small wooden object, like a miniature children's playground slide. It is called an elbow rest. The French saleslady shakes talcum powder into the gloves before putting them on to my outstretched hand, smoothing them over each finger, and gently sliding them up over my small wrist. I wonder if there is any shop in the world today where a sales assistant has been trained to sell a pair of gloves to a ten year old, with such care and attention. Mind you, how many ten year old children would even want anything so posh and daft as unlined delicate leather gloves today? Where on earth would they wear them, even as best? However, I still love the feeling of perfectly fitting unlined leather gloves, even in my eighties - but only for best! Most of the time I pull on my old driving gloves that are getting tattier every year.

My mother is always dressed elegantly, with the help of her skilful Chinese dressmakers, and she loves getting them to make me beautiful little outfits too, including matching hats! Stuart and I always have handmade shoes in Singapore. We are made to stand on a piece of paper in our bare feet, while the shoemaker pencils round our toes and heel, tickling our skin as he does so. I expect all this attention to our clothes and our appearance is forming my adult personality. I care far too much about appearance, and not only my own. Sadly, this means I often judge the book by its cover, and make ridiculous assumptions, until I discover how splendid the book really is!

In England, we always stay with my father's mother, our Nan Hogg, at 110 Hatfield Road, in St Albans. This is a tall Victorian town house, with three floors and a basement. In those days it still has gaslight. My widowed grandmother has made her living as a theatrical landlady, letting out rooms to Variety Artistes who come to appear at the Grand Palace, just round the corner, before it is converted into a cinema. Apart from our family staying at the time, she also has a permanent lodger, Mr Pritchard, as well as her other son and daughter, my uncle Les and Auntie Lena. Uncle Les works for the LMS, (London Midland and Scottish Railway) in some mysterious engineering capacity. Later he is to marry Auntie Rose, and they live in an exciting railway house, built over the tunnel at Finchley Road. I'm not certain what Auntie Lena does, but she has very bad eyesight and wears thick pebble-lensed glasses. In spite of this she also manages to leave home on her marriage, although I seem to remember that no one thought much of the chosen husband.

My mother is very tight-lipped about Nan who has a fairly casual, relaxed attitude to Mummy's favourite philosophies: *Cleanliness is next to Godliness; A stitch in time saves nine; The early bird catches the worm; Strike while the iron's hot*, amongst others. Nan is a free spirit, and spends much of her time reading detective stories and recounting favourite anecdotes about her early life. Ethel Violet Stewart Stephens had spent a short time *on the boards* before becoming a barmaid at a coaching inn at Walthamstow, but she fills me with wonder about *the smell of the grease-paint* and the *lure of the lights*. She loves to play her ancient upright piano, singing all the old music hall favourites. *Oh Mr Porter, what shall I do, I wanted to go to Birmingham, but you've taken me on to Crewe* and *My old man said foller the van and don't dilly dally on the way*. A special favourite is *Knees up Mother Brown, knees up Mother Brown, knees up, knees up don't get the breeze up, knees up Mother Brown.* She plays this faster and faster, singing louder and louder, until my brother and I who try to keep up with her, eventually collapse on the floor in fits of giggles.

She also has an old chocolate box full of cards from all the variety acts that have stayed with her. *To dearest Mum who looked after us so well. All our love.* I find myself thinking it is very strange to call someone Mum or Ma when she isn't their Mum, but accept it as part of that magical world of grownups, especially grownups on the stage. Their messages make it obvious that she is a great favourite with them all.

Every corner of Nan's kitchen has some unique novelty. Seaweed hangs from a hook in one corner, so that we will be able to tell if the next day is going to be wet or dry. To back this up there is a calendar with a picture that turns pink or blue, also depending on the forthcoming weather (no dreary old barometers for our Nan). Suspended from the ceiling in another corner is a hot cross bun kept for many years. I can't remember what superstition surrounds this unhygienic object, but it hangs there gathering dust and germs above an ancient dog called Dido, who lives permanently in an armchair in mounds of cushions, getting older and smellier each day. Hanging from the central gas bracket, is a spiral of flypaper, with a few bodies on it. Below, the big kitchen table, covered with a squashy chenille tablecloth, always has a glass sugar bowl with a net covering, edged with tiny coloured beads that look like fruit gums.

As the light begins to fade, Nan reaches over to the kitchen range with a long taper and then leans over the table to light the gas lamp. First she turns the tap and there is the hiss of the gas coming through, then the touch of the flame to the small bell-shaped mantel, which pops and splutters, turning from bluey-green to pink, and finally glowing bright gold, and the kitchen is ready for high tea. Another treat is holding the long three-pronged toasting fork, in charge of toasting the teacakes or crumpets. There is a high brass fender to lean across, but being able to produce perfectly toasted golden brown teacakes with no burned edges is a moment of pride and joy for us children.

While we are spending those weeks at Nan's, my brother and I also start our first local school. This is a small private school run by the Misses Marian and Isobel Bryce, middle-aged sisters. We enter down some steps into a rather dark cloakroom, where our shoe-bags hang from allocated pegs with our names on. We immediately have to change from our outdoor shoes into our plimsolls, at the same time as we take our coats and hats off and hang them on our peg. Apart from basic lessons of reading, writing and arithmetic, we play gentle games of badminton in the back garden and chase each other in games of tag in the shrubbery. Stuart gets into terrible disgrace for tormenting the girls with stems of nettles on their legs. I remember the gravity of the note my mother receives, reporting on his misconduct. A family forum is held, and poor Stuart is castigated for bullying little girls.

During these first few weeks my parents must have been doing a lot of soul-searching, because gradually we become aware that there is no more talk of interviews at the boarding schools whose prospectuses we'd been examining since before leaving Singapore. Instead the talk is all about our new house which Uncle Tom, Mummy's brother, is going to build for us to 'our own specifications'. Tom is the T in T KING & SON BUILDERS - St Albans' busy and prosperous building firm. I think we must be very grand to have a house built to 'our own specifications'. Mummy says it has to be detached; that she cannot possibly live in a semi-detached house. Actually there is only about six inches between the two new houses he is building, but this seems to satisfy Mummy. It's a pleasant brick-built house of that period, with two reception rooms, three bedrooms, kitchen and bathroom, a large garage and gardens, both back and front. The back leads into a wooded dell which is a mass of bluebells in the spring. The trees are full of noisy crows, but the cuckoos faithfully return to the dell each year, and let us know they are back – "cuckoo".

After leaving Nan and 110 Hatfield Road, we start to settle into 'MALAYSIA', and begin to make friends with new neighbours and make decisions about our new big schools in September. First there is a late summer holiday in Cornwall for two whole weeks. It's our first real English seaside holiday, with long days at the beach, clambering over rocks and investigating rock pools with our shrimping nets, and exploring the beauty of the Cornish countryside. It's also our first introduction to the wonder of Cornish clotted cream teas with scones and strawberry jam. Our landlady at the bed and breakfast makes delicious full cooked breakfasts, packed sandwich lunches, and welcomes us back in the evening with salad high teas: lots of bread and butter and homemade cake. Our parents though are behaving rather strangely, constantly listening to the news on the wireless. Suddenly, at the end of the first week, my father says we have to cancel the rest of the holiday, and drive back to St Albans and our new house. We must start to get some black-out curtains organised, and make our brand new windows shatterproof, with sticky-backed brown paper tape, criss-crossing each pane. I suppose these are the instructions they are listening to over the wireless: instructions given by the BBC news announcers to the entire nation. War has been declared.

Looking back, I realise that my parents' decision to stay with us in England, rather than accepting the usual ex-pat style of life: sending children to boarding school and seeing them so infrequently, is the miracle that kept our family together. If they had returned to Singapore as originally planned, I doubt whether Stuart and I would have seen them again. Most of our adult friends ended up in Changi Jail, or some other prison camp for the duration, and many died, or like our Uncle Norman, became so ill that he died soon after.

I think perhaps this is the first time I have an instinct that there is some sort of

Providence that protects and *shapes our lives, rough hew them as we will* – apologies to Shakespeare. I don't remember having much Christian teaching in Singapore, apart from praying *Gentle Jesus meek and mild, look upon a little child* at bedtime. Daddy went to St Andrews Cathedral occasionally, and I suppose we must have said prayers at school, but God played no positive role in our every-day family life. I'll always remember being so grateful and realising how blessed we are that Mummy and Daddy are with us in England, and not in Singapore with the Japanese.

3

WARTIME – GAS MASKS – AIR RAIDS & SCHOOL

The brand new St Albans Grammar School for Girls is in an impressive modern building. It boasts a magnificent gymnasium, two science laboratories, a well -stocked library, a big bright art room and plenty of grounds for games and athletics. Today it would be considered very run of the mill, but in wartime it is a flagship for education in St Albans, and so off I go to be educated until the age of sixteen: five more years, and for all that time Britain is at war. We are all allocated gas masks in square cardboard boxes, but soon we exchange these for smarter streamlined cases that aren't so bulky to carry about. There is gasmask drill:

"Chins in first girls. Now ease your mask over your ears and hair." The wonderfully rude noises we discover we can make as we breathe out, making the rubber reverberate around our cheeks, causes a lot of disruption as we collapse in hysterical giggles. The sight of us all with our piggy snouts and plastic eye slots are enough to set us all off again in spite of our irritated teachers and their "*Now - come along girls!*" We have air-raid shelter drill as well so that there will never be panic at the eerie wailing sound of the siren. On the back of our desks we have special shoulder bags containing our gas mask, a torch, a bottle of fresh water or juice and something to eat in case we have to stay underground in the shelters for many hours. When the siren goes there has to be complete silence, then each row stands up one at a time by their desks with their shoulder bags and outdoor jackets. Still in silence we parade out to the nearest designated exit, across the playground in single file to the allotted shelter. Down the cement steps into the cold gloomy tunnel with wooden forms along each side, and hurricane lamps a few yards distance from each other. These are lit by one of our teachers when we are all sitting down. So much school time is wasted though, as more often than not, having settled everyone down the All Clear will sound. It's the same procedure in reverse back to our classrooms.

One momentous day I'm told that I have been chosen to broadcast a message to all the children of Russia who have just become our allies in the war. No one tells me who has made this rather grandiose decision and as I am only thirteen at the time, I just accept it. A train journey to St Pancras in wartime is a great treat, as all school trips to London are cancelled because of the air raids. I am handed a small scrap of paper (today now yellow with age) with this typewritten message:

"We the pupils of St Albans Grammar School for Girls send our love and greetings to the girls and boys of the Soviet Union. We are proud to know that your great country is united with ours in this struggle for freedom,

and we hope that the bonds of friendship which are now being forged between our two nations will become ever stronger, so that when this dreadful war is over, we can work together to build a better world and prevent the repetition of the agony and suffering which so many people are undergoing today. Our school motto is NOBIS CURA FUTURI which means OUR CARE IS FOR THE FUTURE and we want to do all we can to prepare ourselves to take our part as citizens in the brave new world which we are determined shall arise out of the sufferings and sacrifices of today."

It's on the back of a school medical certificate (saving paper) and I virtually know it off by heart by the time we set off on the historic journey. Immaculate in my royal blue and gold school uniform, and for once correctly wearing my navy blue velour hat with the school crest, long black lisle stockings and highly polished shoes, we set off.

The BBC studio is at Kingsway Hall off The Strand, but all I remember of the visit is the excitement of being put in the care of one of the famous wartime news announcers, Mr Alvar Liddell. He seems to me to be so tall and kind and encouraging as he takes me to the microphone and shows me where to stand, not too close and not too far, and then I read the message that one of our school staff has written. It sounds highly reminiscent of one of Winston Churchill's to my ears today. I wonder what the Russian schoolchildren thought of it all those many years ago.

As schoolchildren there are regular visits to our great Abbey Church, built to commemorate the death of Alban, the first Christian martyr in England in the third century. I love being asked to read the lesson and feel so excited standing high up on the lectern, which is in the shape of a great golden eagle, peering over the top of his wings at all the upturned faces down the length of that great nave which has been standing since 1077.

I remember so many of those teachers with great affection, and realise how they encouraged me in speech and drama, giving me a love for art and music, and feeding my imagination for story telling. In particular, Miss Mitchell our scripture teacher has this very special gift with an ability to sow seeds into at least one of her rapt listeners. Her telling of the story of Saul's journey on the Damascus Road resonates with life for me. The fact that Jesus actually spoke to Saul gives me a longing to hear Jesus speak to me too. At home in the privacy of my bedroom, I stand and lean out of my window to make sure no-one is around and pray "Dear Jesus, please will you give me a Damascus Road experience as you did with St Paul. I want to be used like you used him. Amen." Even then my belief that prayers are answered stems from the fact that I was always losing things and rather than being constantly lectured by my parents, I secretly ask Jesus to find them. He nearly always does. The Damascus road prayer will be answered one day in the far distant future. Not in the way I expected, and at the time, I never realise that a small seed has been sown during that scripture lesson at school

Perhaps it's the experience of being upfront during all those early days of my life that inspires my growing desire to communicate to people, although I don't connect it with theatre or acting, having never seen a professional play with actors in it. Because of the war, schools are unable to visit the London theatres, unlike schools today. Added to this, my parents aren't really interested in the arts so I miss any encouragement at home. The first illuminating spark that lights up the magic of acting for me is a sixth form production of G B Shaw's "St Joan". I am inspired by Jeanne d'Arc and her passionate belief that God has spoken to her through her voices, and I identify with her, especially in the trial scene. Joan is sitting on a low stool, alone, surrounded by the massed power and authority of England. She leaps to her feet crying defiantly:

"Give me that paper, light your fires. Do you think I dread it as much as the life of a rat in a hole? My voices were right. They told

me that you were fools and that I was not to listen to your fine words nor trust to your charity." Like her I am prepared to face martyrdom, to walk out to the fire and challenge the world. Now I know what I'm going to do. In the school library the next day I find those plays of Mr George Bernard Shaw. There are so many more of his books, but at last I find "St Joan". And there is the trial scene and *that* speech. I spend my lunch hour copying it out to make it mine. I decide to learn it by heart so that I can perform it somehow, somewhere, sometime to thrill an audience, as I have been thrilled. It's also the subject matter that captures me. Her passionate beliefs are so big, so important, overriding all the trivialities of our daily lives. I want those too. I don't know the girl who played St Joan, or whether her performance would have merited any medals, I just know she becomes the catalyst for my longing to act. Like her I long to move an audience to tears, to make them laugh, to carry them into the magical world of imagination. I determine to live my own life as uncompromisingly as St

Joan's. The lure of theatre lights takes the place of the light on the Damascus Road.

4

RADA AND WARTIME LONDON

My first steps away from the leafy suburbs of Hertfordshire are taken along the streets of Bloomsbury from St Pancras station to Gower Street. At last I find myself outside the pillared entrance of THE ROYAL ACADEMY OF DRAMATIC ART. The excitement of passing my entrance audition (which includes the speech from St Joan) is only overtaken by the first morning. I step up into the black and white marble-floored hall where so many famous actors have stood and talked, and learned their craft. At only just sixteen I find it all overwhelming. In comparison with most of the students there I am a very immature and unsophisticated teenager. I still wear my navy blue gabardine school raincoat to RADA each day and often feel very out of place. I start two weeks late due to illness, and immediately chum up with a girl whose first day also coincides with mine. She is blonde with a husky voice and explains it is her 'gin & fog' voice. She tells endless stories about her French lover in the Maquis (the Underground Resistance in France) and has a suite at Claridges hotel paid for by her father. I find her irresistibly glamorous. She isn't beautiful, just chic with lots of eye make-up. After much persuasion from her I agree to have an evening out together, and she drags me off to a West End restaurant in Piccadilly Circus - The Criterion. We climb up a long crimson and gold-carpeted staircase where a waiting attendant in wine and gold livery and a top hat takes our coats; mine is my school raincoat. We are then ushered to a table for two and when the waiter asks us to order our drinks, I wait for Elizabeth. She nonchalantly orders lager, so I nonchalantly order one as well, although I have no idea what it tastes like. As I look around it seems that romantic couples in service uniform occupy every table. Perhaps they are having a few precious days with each other, on leave from the battlefront, or even on honeymoon. My schoolgirl imagination makes up romantic scenarios for all those tables. Most evenings my parents insist I come home immediately after college - and never any later than ten. Admittedly, I am only just sixteen and the war is still on. Although there are now far fewer air raids, there are still the buzz bombs. These are missiles sent across the channel. At first you hear the buzz of their engines, but when these suddenly cut out, that's the moment to dive for cover.

Sadly I make very little impact at RADA. I have a lot of fun with my classmates; and one or two of them make names for themselves. Roger Moore is one, the son of a London policeman. He has enormous good looks and great charm. Soon after leaving RADA he is starring in the television series

"The Saint," and later as 007, taking over from Sean Connery. Then there is Lois Maxwell a Canadian student who becomes Miss Moneypenny, also in the James Bond films.

It seems to me that I need to have the confidence that Elizabeth has from wealth and social position, or that something we now call street-cred - which Roger has. I don't have either. I am just middle of the road. I haven't as yet discovered who I am, what special qualities I possess, if any, and I certainly have no idea how to exploit them. I am slightly plump, well behaved, anxious to please, and probably seem to be very unpromising material. For our Shakespeare play "Romeo and Juliet", instead of one of the wonderful love scenes which I long to play, I am given the highly emotional scene where Juliet is in the family tomb terrified, just before taking Friar Lawrence's potion. This has me in such an emotional state; I spend the whole afternoon in tears, and have to be comforted by all my older classmates. Mainly I am cast as middle-aged character parts with padding everywhere, mortified with embarrassment. Two years later after struggling to keep up with my peers, my parents receive the letter that says the staff of RADA feel I am temperamentally unsuited to the demanding life of an actress, implying that I will be too easily hurt by its inevitable rejections along the way. They will never know that after the first bitter disappointment and painful tears I am more determined than ever to stay in the business, and to learn my skills by actually acting somehow, somewhere. I know I have the temperament that reacts more positively to seemingly impossible situations. The more people tell me *it cannot be done,* the more determined I become to show them *yes it can.* Perhaps it's also this streak of stubbornness that is to stand me in good stead after Adam's murder all those years later and eventually, to make 'The Choice'....

My determination to ignore the prognosis of RADA's well-intentioned advisors hits a snag to begin with. My parents step in and declare that I must have a second string to my bow. This means starting immediately after the summer holidays at the local Secretarial College, run by two elderly ladies, where I am to learn Pitman's shorthand and accompanying typing skills. I'm furious, but realise this is the only way they will allow me to launch myself into the unknown dangers of the stage. I borrow an ancient typewriter and continue to practice typing at home. I am determined to get the necessary speeds, so that I can leave as soon as possible. Looking back I realise that having this year off allows destiny to step in and re-order my future for me.

I join the local amateur Drama Club which has an excellent reputation, and I am immediately given some wonderful parts. My evenings spent rehearsing and getting to know some very talented members of the company are enormous fun. They are a much needed respite from the shorthand and typing classes under the formidable principals – Miss House and Miss Williams.

Through the drama group I begin to regain my confidence because of being given characters that are so much closer to my own age and personality. I also start to grow up and feel that I belong; that the others in the group believe in me and in any talent I have. I make some very good friends, get the requisite speeds at college, and am able to show my parents that if necessary I can actually hold a job as a secretary. It's a very happy phase of my life and an essential growing time for my future stage career.

Each year there's a week's festival for some of the best drama groups around the country to compete with a selection of one-act plays. I am chosen to play a young country girl, looking after her wounded grandfather, who has just returned from the battle of Waterloo. While she's busy making his tea, they get a visit from a senior officer bearing a letter from Queen Victoria, awarding the old regular soldier something equivalent to the Victoria Cross. There are just the three characters, and it's a shameless weepie, which the large enthusiastic audience loves. Each night a programme of three one-act plays is performed by drama groups from all over the UK. At the end of the week the adjudicator gives his breathlessly awaited comments and final awards for the best production and performance - a mini Oscar evening. Sitting in the crowded auditorium I can hardly believe my ears when I hear the sentence that is going to change my whole career:

"Out of the entire week, I will always remember the performance of the young woman in "Waterloo" – for her moving and professional acting."

It's the word professional I hug to my heart. I am a professional actress. I have always known I was. Now no one is going to stop me. I settle down to find out more about this man who is changing my life. I discover he is a West End Producer, a theatrical entrepreneur, and he lives in Eton. Very soon he is going to get a letter from me. I tell him I have been at RADA for two years, but am having difficulty finding my first job. Is there any chance he can help me? I will never forget his reply: *"However talented any actor or actress might be, not even a Peggy Ashcroft or*

Sybil Thorndike or even the great Edith Evans, will ever persuade me that the world of theatre is not the most heart-breaking life anyone can undertake." Therefore on principle he will not help me to get that first job. However, if I ignore his advice and make that break through on my own - then I can come back to him. Clinging to this promise and with the help of two very special friends already in the business, I find myself travelling by rail with one of our large cabin trunks to Liverpool, and across to Northern Ireland for a year's contract with the Belfast Arts Theatre. The journey has begun....

5

BELFAST ARTS THEATRE

I'm on the first rung of the ladder, and going away for a whole year to rep in the 1950s means I need to take everything I possess in my wardrobe. Every small accessory: gloves, scarves, shoes, and dress jewellery. We are responsible for all our modern costumes, so it is essential to have an extensive wardrobe. Some managements choose their leading ladies solely because of their elegant clothes. One of the family's much travelled cabin trunks is filled to the brim, and with high expectations off I go to Belfast and my new stage career. I'm on my own - on my way, and on the boat train to Liverpool. I've booked a cabin on the night ferry to Belfast docks, arriving first thing the next morning. A friendly young Scotsman is waiting on the quayside to take me first to my digs and then to the theatre. He is mainly working on stage management, with the occasional chance of smaller parts. We soon become firm friends. In those days there is no Actors Equity Union, in Northern Ireland, and Ian is paid just enough to keep him as he learns his way into the business. He seems to be doing every job in the theatre including cleaning. When he isn't in the current play, he even sells programmes.

Up some narrow stairs over a printing firm, we find the small Belfast Arts Theatre. Suddenly we are in a very attractive lobby. This is also the box office and coffee bar - and the domain of Dorothy Wilmott the director's wife. She rules it with rigour. My main memory of Dorothy that still remains with me is her pristine appearance, with high heels and tight skirts, and her black pencilled eyebrows, which make her look fierce. It's a warning to us all. Her tolerance level for the pranks of the young is virtually nil. We soon learn to watch it when Dorothy is around. Hibby (or Hubert Wilmott) is our overall Artistic Director. He's a fidgety man, always rattling coins in his trouser pockets; in his forties, with a nervous laugh and stammer. He wears large horn-rimmed spectacles, and loves brightly coloured shirts and flamboyant ties and cravats. Apart from his rather eccentric appearance and manner, he is very shrewd and acquires the Irish rights to plays still running in the West End or on Broadway and even in Europe. Many of our posters proudly announce IRISH PREMIERE of... and this is the reason that the literati and professional classes in Belfast flock to see his productions. My salary is £6.00 a week and my theatre digs £2.10s. in old money, with three home-cooked meals each day, so the rest is pocket money. A complete meal in a Belfast restaurant is 2/6d (half a crown) or the equivalent of 25p. And if I suddenly discover some unexpected larger items, there's always my Post Office Savings Book. My parents have always encouraged me to have a little nest egg for rainy days.

"Six Characters in Search of an Author" by Pirandello is my first play, and I am playing the female lead. It is an enormous part and wonderfully rewarding. However Hibby seems to have no idea about directing either the play, or his actors. I have nightmares about his ineptitude; with all of us standing in straight rows mouthing lines which none of us understand. I can still hear him saying, after one of us questions him about the meaning of a line, "Oh no one's going to understand what it's all about so just play it for all you're worth, and they'll think it's great. I haven't an idea what it's all about." We are all dressed in black and I give a madly dramatic performance. I'm certain it's dreadful.

We all meet the morning after the first night to have coffee, quickly grabbing the morning papers to see what they have made of the whole evening. To my amazement the Belfast theatre critic's review sports the headline BETTY MOST DESERVED AN AUTHOR. (Beth came quite a few years later). I float on air, until further down I read some more flattering remarks about another actor that I know are totally undeserved. This brings me back to reality, and obviously Hibby is right: *they haven't a clue!*

My year at The Arts is a gift beyond value. I am being thrown in at the deep end, as I'm playing enormous parts in amazing plays with each play running for about a month. After Pirandello, I start learning the lines for Isabelle, the lead in Anouilh's "Ring Round the Moon". I'd seen it in London, with the beautiful Claire Bloom and Paul Schofield in the two demanding leads. They were both enchanting in this romantic and lyrical comedy of the fifties, directed by the inspirational Peter Brook; so when I read in the Belfast press that they think our performances are better, I know never to take them seriously again. Playing the young ballerina who is desperately in love with the aristocratic Hugo, who treats her with such disdain, gives me the chance of passionately declaring my love, in one emotional speech which nearly reduces me to real tears each night.

"The Glass Menagerie" is my next invaluable leading part as Tennessee

Williams' painfully introvert Laura, being dressed up by her Mother ready to meet *the gentleman caller*. Each night being given false bosoms as Laura, I remember all the hurt and rejection I'd experienced when I was sixteen at RADA, when I knew I couldn't keep up with everyone's expectations of me. Now I realise I know how Laura feels. "The Glass Menagerie" has a tenderness that I understand so well.

After fifty years I still have some little glass animals from that production, given to me by an actor called James Ellis, who at that time is just back from The Bristol Old Vic School, and who plays my *gentleman caller*. He is twenty-one, with all the charm that Ireland so often invests in her people. Six feet tall, all arms and legs with an infectious grin and an anarchic sense of humour. His charismatic talent make our scenes together magical. This is a wonderful way to start falling in love. On tour for four weeks round the beautiful six counties, travelling in the back of the van along with the set and furniture, snuggled together with rugs to keep warm, I am already in love with him. The tour becomes our weeks of '*courtin*' - full of wonder and fun. The people in those small market towns are some of the friendliest I will ever meet. They have such a concern for our welfare. After the show they want to meet us and talk, and tables are laid out, loaded with delicious homemade pastries and cakes of every kind. They think young actors need to be fed having given their all, and actors are *always* ravenous. We all come back for more, balancing a cup of tea or coffee in one hand, and saying all the right things to all those lovely people at the same time.

Portstewart, one of Northern Ireland's coastal towns, not far from The Giant's Causeway, becomes a pivotal moment for me on that tour. Here, during the day, as we are climbing over the rocks on the shore, playing like children throwing pebbles into pools, snug in our winter coats and scarves, I suddenly hug myself thinking: '*This is the life I've chosen. I'm being paid for all this joy, and tonight I have the task to make a little magic on an unknown stage for all those people who are sitting out there. I am so fortunate to be doing just what I want to do. How many people can say that?'* Sitting on one of the rocks, watching the others larking about, basking in all the beauty of that coast, and the choppy Irish Sea stretching all the way across to Norway. That first year's testing of the waters is to prove my life-long love of the theatre, and for Northern Ireland's beauty and its friendly people.

At the end of my year's contract I return to England, and follow up my first letter to Jack Minster in Eton, who is true to his word, and introduces me to the current director of Windsor's Theatre Royal, Hugh Cruttwell, just married to Geraldine McEwan, who is now fondly remembered as Miss Marple on our TV sets. Hugh and I have tea at one of Eton's tea shops, and while chatting, I interrupt anxiously, "Will you give me an audition to see if I can act?"

"No, I'm not in favour of auditions on the whole. Never think people give of their best; it's an artificial situation. I can usually tell just by talking to someone if they have that special something." My heart sinks into my boots. I haven't been trying to impress.

"So how does one get that special something?" He grins at my discomfort.

"How do you know you haven't got it?"

Thanking him for meeting me, and for my tea and cakes, I get the train back to London in misery. I'm sharing a flat in Swiss Cottage with another actress from Belfast, and tell her all about this lovely meeting, but am certain it is a non-event. In just over a week, a large envelope arrives in my post with a script in it, and a letter from Mr Cruttwell offering me a part in the next play. Would I be interested? Of course! Apparently I do have that special something.

This is my first UK opportunity. The play, "Wishing Well", is a light romantic love story set in a Welsh village. I am the daughter of the local postmaster, desperately in love with the local schoolmaster. He is also desperately in love with me, but feels unable to say yes to marriage. He's temporarily in a wheelchair due to an accident, and being scrupulously worthy, feels he would only be an encumbrance. Eventually by Act III, my faith in his recovery is answered...and we live happily ever after. Patrick McGoohan is the incredibly handsome actor who plays my loved one. We travel from Waterloo to Windsor each day, Patrick burying his nose in a book, daring me to make small talk with him. It takes time, but eventually he comes out of his shell and I relish our scenes with each other. He loves hearing me talk about Ireland and my love for the people, but is full of derision about his own career, "I'm thinking of giving it all up. I'll buy a chicken farm in Ireland." However television series such as "Danger Man" and "The Visitor" amongst others, bring film offers from Hollywood. Sadly for us, he leaves our shores to live there. Working with that seriously honest actor is a special joy for me. "Wishing Well" is a very 1950s, middle class, middle-aged, slight, nonsense play. Windsor loves it, and in the audience a London agent loves me, and puts me on his books. However, in spite of his swish office in Regent Street and his many contacts, I soon discover that Freddie wants a little more than merely promoting my career. I can't handle this, and soon return to Belfast.

Who could resist playing the wonderful part of Judith Bliss in Coward's "Hayfever?"

Laura in Tenessee William's 'The Glass Menagerie'.

'Actor Managers' - signing the book in the Mayor's parlour in Bangor Co Down.

Diana and I as Cecily and Gwendoline in "The Importance of Being Earnest"

Happy days - our wedding at St Albans Abbey

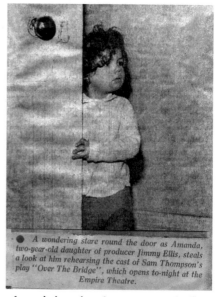

A wondering stare round the door as *Amanda*, two-year-old daughter of producer *Jimmy Ellis*, steals a look at him rehearsing the cast of Sam Thompson's play "Over The Bridge", which opens to-night at the Empire Theatre.

A very proud Dad with Amanda, his first granddaughter home at St Albans

Amanda busy keeping an eye on Dad's rehearsals for "Over the Bridge"

Baby Hugo has joined us - an armful of three.

16 Holland Park Avenue - Jimmy the new star of BBC's "Z Cars"

A radiant Amanda and Mother of the bride at the reception.

Ladbroke Square Gardens and Bruce Collins at Hugo and Rachel's wedding.

Another happy bride Rachel and Hugo with both Mums and Dads.

6

ACTOR MANAGERS-BANGOR CO.DOWN

I find Belfast's Arts Theatre is still doing new West End Releases and The Ulster Group Theatre is concentrating on Ulster kitchen comedies. Both theatres rehearse for two to three weeks, and sometimes play for a month. In the seaside resort of Bangor Co. Down however, the first professional weekly rep company has been formed. Margery Mason, a London actress in her mid forties, has been persuaded to be its first professional Artistic Director. Margery first asks James Ellis, whom I now call Jimmy, and then me, to join her company. We begin a few weeks before the big Christmas pantomime, getting ourselves attuned to the fast weekly rehearsals and turnover. Then comes the panto with its dozens of excited child dancers dressed up as fairies. As always the pantomime brings in full houses. Jimmy is thoroughly enjoying himself as one of the Ugly Sisters, brilliantly outlandish, knowing the audience is loving his performance. I am a very stylish Prince Charming in glittering silver tunic and principal boy tights, with the highest of heels. Sadly I have to open my mouth to sing!

Working in weekly rep is a tough system, a system that has virtually disappeared today. The first play of the season is the easiest, you have the full week to learn your lines and rehearse. From the second week onwards you're performing one play at night, and rehearsing a totally different play, creating a completely new character during the day. Audiences find it totally puzzling,

"Don't you ever get mixed up as to which play you're doing?"

"Well once you get into the routine and are very disciplined about going home to learn your lines, after the curtain comes down it becomes a habit."

The wise director always tries to vary the parts each week, so that no actor finds they are playing one enormous part after another. Sadly the pantomime is going to be our last show. All our jobs are ending. The theatre is closing – going dark. Margery has been running the theatre virtually single-handed for over a year, and is exhausted. She's longing to get back home to London for a well-deserved rest before pursuing her own acting career. As Jimmy and I are still together, our future is looking bleak. I will have to go back to England to find my next job and leave Jimmy here in Ulster. We are trying to work this out for ourselves not realising that life, with a capital L is working it out for us behind the scenes.

A group of theatre enthusiasts in Bangor wholeheartedly give their time quite voluntarily, sometimes working both night and day to make sure that they can boast of their very own professional theatre. Mrs Hanna is one of these. She has worked tirelessly with Margery wherever she is needed in the Front of House. She appears to be responsible for ordering all the cakes and biscuits for the coffee bar, and is often the friendly face in the box office. In fact, she is invaluable. Apart from all this, she makes sure that the members of the company are spoiled and looked after at weekends, with delicious home-cooked meals. Her apple cake and cream is from heaven above. Hers is the sort of cooking I've never tasted better anywhere else other than from those wonderful Mums of Northern Ireland. With silver grey hair and the bluest of eyes, she mothers us all. One evening in the coffee bar after the show she beckons me over, whispering conspiratorially... "Could we have a wee chat Beth?" Then having sat us both down in a quiet corner, she continues. "Beth, the committee who look after the coffee bar, the box office, and the programme sellers are all devastated that Margery's leaving us, and we'll be losing our own wee theatre."

"I know Mrs Hanna, and we're so sad to be leaving you all. We've loved being here. You've been so kind." I take both her hands in mine trying to comfort her.

"Well Beth, we were wondering, would you not consider taking over from Margery yourself?" I am flabbergasted.

"Me, Mrs Hanna?" My first reaction is of course not. I am a twenty-six year old actress with no notion of the daily running of a theatre. My training at RADA was purely as a performer. She is so persuasive however, telling me that all the others also feel complete confidence in me. Naturally, I feel very flattered, so I add rather weakly, "Well now, Mrs Hanna why don't I have a wee chat with Jimmy, see what he thinks." In the 21st century this sounds totally feeble, but remember, we were still in the fifties, before mini-skirts and the gender revolution of the sixties. It never occurs to me that I can take on this responsibility. Definitely not without a man to help and support me! In total wonderment I go and tell Jimmy.

"What do you mean; we don't know how to run a theatre? We'll learn as we go long. What an opportunity darling. You have to be an opportunist in this business. Of course, we'll take it on. Go back and say yes." So I go back, with our answer.

"Thank you, Mrs Hanna - we'll have a go." She hugs me to her bosom in delight. Good news travels fast. Immediately Jimmy is in touch with his great friend from school and college days, James Greene, another actor, working at Belfast's Arts Theatre. All of Belfast's writers, poets, painters, and actors know each other. We all eat in the same pub. Especially, we all drink together. We are all of an age, with aspirations to talk over, ambitions to share. This news is great crack, and many drinks are consumed in the many bars in Belfast, over the forthcoming plans. We are the new generation. We are going to do exciting new plays the moment they're released. We can use the Front of House for art exhibitions, and all our artist friends will help us refurbish the theatre in exchange. There's such a buzz in the bars of Belfast, as we sit sharing our dreams together. No one of our age has ever been given a theatre to run. Now we aren't just actors – but Actor - Managers. Not even Laurence Olivier at The National Theatre can have known the thrill we have at this opportunity.

I am totally won over by such Irish enthusiasm, but first - the practicalities. Finance, for instance, needs to be sorted out. Thankfully the owner of the theatre, Tom Bailey, once also a popular Mayor of Bangor, just happens to be related to Mrs Hanna, and her daughter is married to Tom's son. I soon discover that Tom is as delighted as Mrs Hanna that Bangor is still going to have its own theatre, and that he will be the one responsible for taking a chance with us. I'm left wondering how much chat has been going on behind the scenes....

We decide we are to be a tri-partite directorship: the two Jims and me. Jimmy will be the Artistic Director; Jim Greene, our handsome Leading Man. I will be Leading Lady and general dog's-body, and our Juvenile Lead is to be Diana: petite, dark-haired, with an attractive husky voice, and currently performing at 'The Arts' in Belfast.

First we must meet with Mr Tom Bailey, this trusting saviour of ours. His estate agents office is next door to the theatre. We have often met him before and seen him around Bangor. The theatre is part of the building that includes his office. I believe it was originally used as a warehouse and storage, before some bright spark thought about converting the space into a theatre, seating just two hundred and twenty. Sitting the three of us down, he leans forward onto his desk, asking us to put forward all our suggestions.

"Now then, you just tell me your needs and I'll do all I can to help you." He is a darling man, in his sixties, with a full head of white hair, and bright blue eyes that have a definite twinkle. He really wants his son William to take over the estate agents business, so that he can enjoy himself with all his other interests. One of these includes an attractive country-house hotel, a few miles along the coast, opposite a cluster of islands called The Copelands.

Suddenly he broaches a most unexpected suggestion. Would I be interested in being his manageress there, while we are getting the theatre re-furbished? This means that I will no longer have to pay rent at my flat. It's a brilliant idea. He gets an unpaid manageress keeping an eye on the hotel in the slow months of January and February, and I will have a very nice place to live in without paying rent. As there's only one bus each hour and none of us owns a car, he makes it quite clear that we can have all our directors' meetings at the hotel, with meals entirely at his expense. There are no strings attached with Tom. We have long discussions with him over budgets. He knows his way around business finance far better than any of us. We will try to manage with a basic central team of ten. Someone needs to go to London to find three more actors older than us, to play the character parts. Tom instantly suggests he will pay Jimmy's fares as he's overall Artistic Director, to contact some London agents. The end of March in just three months' time becomes our suggested deadline for getting everything together for Opening Night. The painting and decorating begins.

I am Mr Bailey's manageress at The

Copelands Hotel, Donaghadee. This small fishing village is two miles further along the coast road. The steel grey Irish skies match a grey choppy sea. My large double bedroom with its enormous bay windows is at the front of the hotel, overlooking the sea and the islands, which are only inhabited by rabbits and birds. The windows are more often than not soaked with the slanting wind-driven rain coming in directly from the angry Irish Sea. Looking out at it I feel so exhilarated by this wild bleak view of the coastline. The turbulent sea and sky feel as if they might invade the hotel, devouring everything, including me.

I've not been given much of a job description by anyone. I just try to keep everything looking as spic and span as possible, working alongside the small resident winter staff of four. I hardly ever see the chef, a young man in his first job after training college, apart from a friendly chat early each morning about his proposed daily menu. The pretty chambermaid brings my fully cooked Irish three-course breakfast to my room on a tray each morning. This consists of cereal, followed by bacon, egg, tomato and delicious potato bread, finishing with toast and marmalade and coffee. She is bubbly and friendly, from the village, and we chat happily together.

I'm not certain what their boss Mr Bailey has told the staff about my job here, but I notice they are friendly, up to a limit. Ted is Head Waiter or maitre d'hotel. He has a very high opinion of his position in the hotel, and although there's absolutely nothing to do on the days we have no bookings for lunch, he disdains to do anything outside his sphere as maitre d. I quite unintentionally put my foot in it one particularly dreary day, suggesting that the windows in the lounge can do with a good clean, and perhaps he and I can have a go at them together. He is shocked and talks about his position and his Trade Union rules, and says that it is entirely outside his job description. I'm amazed, having come from a profession where if there's a need, you help out. Anyway, as soon as I realise my mistake, I apologise to dear Ted and set about the windows on my own. I thoroughly enjoy the evenings when we have people in for a meal, or just a drink, chatting to them and making them feel welcome. It's a very happy couple of months for me, thanks to Tom Bailey's generosity.

In Bangor everything is coming together for the celebrity-laden First Night Opening of our theatre. Apart from trying out the role of hotel manageress for the very first time, my theatre dog's-body bit is also proving a steep learning curve! I research everything I can find about those literary agents who publish play lists. I learn about performing-rights for any music we play; start writing publicity blurbs for the local Belfast papers, and broadcast an interview on the Belfast BBC "Woman's Hour," going out all over the UK.

"How does it feel running your own theatre?"

OH...WOW! We're buzzing with the challenge.

The invitations go out to members of the Arts Council, local Ulster Government, BBC Directors, the Press, and every celebrity we can muster between us. We find there's a great deal of interest in our budding little theatre and its enthusiastic but as yet untried, youthful management. Everyone accepts...

The first night fulfils our highest expectations. Critics and audience alike are delighted with "Captain Carvallo", our choice of play, but even more so with us, the new young untested company. Once the curtain is down we quickly join the audience, and find the bar humming with the many celebrities we have invited. We get the mandatory; "Darlings you were all wonderful." The future looks exciting.

Jimmy has persuaded some talented young actors just beginning their careers to join us. Julian Glover, straight from RADA is a real find. In "The Lady's not for Burning", playing Humphrey, and boldly seducing my Jennet Jourdemayne, I well remember his arms pinning me to the wall, and the kiss that follows. Oh Julian! – a thrill each night. A great team member too. Sitting in the auditorium, he watches Jimmy as he is directing the two youngest members of the company in a very tender love scene. Julian sidles up to me, "Your old man has just been working wonders with those two in that scene – what a director!" Sadly we lose him too soon, as the Royal Shakespeare Theatre make him an offer to join them in their new season.

Another emerging talent of the time is from Bangor itself. Colin Blakely, from a well-known Ulster family, and around the same age as us, has recently made a great personal hit with critics in London, as part of the Bangor Drama Club, in a one-act play festival. We suggest he plays the same part with us. "Rope" – a tensely written thriller, is perfect for the first half of the evening, and we will repeat our recent production of "The Browning Version" for the second half. The theatre is a sell-out. All of Colin's fans are there, as well as most of Bangor and the local Drama Club. We're adding another talented actor to our circle of friends.

Colin starts coming round to our flat after the show. I make a pot of porridge as a cheap and easy supper, leaving Jimmy and him talking theatre, and then I slip off to bed to learn lines for next week's show. After a slow start in the early months, audiences start to grow. It becomes second nature to me to count the seats at the curtain call each night, and we finally arrive at that wonderful week when I can go to Tom and Mrs. Hanna to announce, "Tom, the box office receipts are enough and more to pay all the bills. Thank you so very much for covering all our debts. Hopefully we won't need to come to you again." He is thrilled for us. Not just about the money, I know that's secondary with him. He just wants us to prove him right. He is a darling man.

"The Importance of Being Earnest" fills the theatre for *two* weeks. Everyone says that classic period plays are always a failure. It's an anniversary for Oscar Wilde, so we take a chance. The costumes from Bermans costumiers in London are magnificent. We decide to get individual photographs of each member of the cast in these eye-catching costumes. Then we borrow gilt frames from

Woolworth's hard-working manager, and finally persuade every shop from the railway station, down the Main Street, to the very end, at the sea front, to display them in their windows along with our theatre display card. The publicity works – for both weeks.

After this production, Jim and Diana decide to get married in Bangor's local church, feeling the time has come to move on and start a family. This leaves Jimmy and me with a predicament. In the fifties, and particularly in a small Ulster town like Bangor, it isn't seemly for two well-known and well-liked members of its theatre company to be flagrantly *living in sin,* and it could reflect on Tom and everyone else who are backing us. It was acceptable when all four of us were sharing the flat, but now...? We need to be married. How on earth can we find the time to get away? The answer is heaven sent. A rather famous local film actor and playwright, Joseph Tomelty, has been recovering from a severe car accident sustained while filming "The Snows of Kilimanjaro" with Ava Gardner. Out of the blue he sends Jimmy the first play he's written since his recovery. He wants to make his comeback, with Jimmy directing: in Bangor with our company. Again the theatre will be filled for the necessary two weeks, and it needs an Irish cast. I am redundant!

"So, my darling, would you like to use the weeks to finally get married?" I don't remember any bended knee. It is October 1958. At last I shall be respectably married. I am twenty-eight, and himself is twenty-six. Ringing my parents, we give them the exciting news that we are coming home to St Albans to get married in our beautiful cathedral, with two nights in a London hotel for our honeymoon. My parents' first reaction is delight, and then horror, when I say we will be organizing this in a couple of weeks' time. When my mother begins to protest, I point out to her that we only want a very few friends and close family. Could she organise a little party at home afterwards and book some tickets for a Drury Lane musical in the evening? Daddy is to book a hotel for the two nights for us, so what could be simpler than that?

The weather on the day is warm and sunny. My fifties style pale blue and silver taffeta ballerina-length dress, with its multitude of stiffened petticoats is the perfect choice. Jimmy's mother makes sure that her son has an appropriate grey suit for the big event, but his parents aren't able to fly over and join us. Looking back I realise how sad this will have been for them. Our service is in the Lady Chapel of St Albans Abbey, small enough to accommodate our few guests without them feeling over-whelmed. I'm surprised how nervous I am. My legs keep trembling as we stand at the altar. Surely being on stage week after week, I should take this without a tremor. I look at Jimmy, wondering how nervous he must be with all this unaccustomed Anglican splendour, and with so few friends of his own to support him.

Returning to Bangor as Mr and Mrs Ellis, weekly rep continues with our faithful team of actors. As the winter months progress, we face various hazards. One night, there is an electricity breakdown all over town. Do we have to cancel that evening's performance? Our Tom Bailey has an answer. Not only has he been Mayor of Bangor, he is also on the board of the local cottage hospital. We perform with the help of Hurricane lamps borrowed for the evening, along with oil lamps and candles in the coffee bar. Thankfully no Health and Safety inspectors are around in the 1950s.

Later in the spring, we discover I am gloriously pregnant, with a baby due the following October. We are both thrilled, but start to recognise that the time is coming to begin making plans to move on. One of the final plays I'm in is a thriller, in which I get thrown around the stage. Justin, the landlord of our flat, is also a young doctor in a Belfast hospital. He urges us to think seriously about my growing baby, suggesting that this might do some irreparable harm. We take this to heart and summon up courage to have a final talk with Tom and Mrs Hanna. They have been so generous, and encouraged us every step of the way. When we tell them our news though, they also share in our delight. It's very emotional; we explain we have to tell the actors that all our jobs are coming to an end. The lights at The New Theatre Bangor will go dark in another month's time. However, having run our own theatre for the last eighteen months is to prove an invaluable experience for us both in the future. We have learned so much and made so many new friends who will be happy to employ Jimmy and me.

Belfast BBC immediately employs Jimmy in various radio plays, and the Ulster Group theatre directors are pleased that he is free to join them again. I enjoy being a lady of leisure – going for pre-natal checks, and reading everything I can find on maternity care. Eventually, Jimmy feels he wants to explore the possibilities of getting work further afield - hopefully in London.

7

BIRTH OF AMANDA-'OVER THE BRIDGE'

Back in England, we live with my parents to begin with, until we then find our first small flat in London. Mr and Mrs James Ellis have their first married home on the first floor of one of those large Victorian houses in Swiss Cottage. On the floor above, a concert pianist practices glorious Chopin nearly all day long. I lie on the sofa convinced that Chopin will surely influence our baby, as she lays curled up in my womb.

I clamber each week to the top of Hampstead Heath High Street, to the natal clinic in the small maternity hospital called Queen Mary's, where Amanda has been booked in. It was originally named after the wife of King George Vth and built specifically for the wives of officers serving abroad. In the fifties it is considered a jewel in the crown, forward-looking in its approach and with a hand-picked staff. My midwife's care for me is something I will never forget. I am doubly blessed as Jimmy is with me at Amanda's birth, rubbing my back copiously, and worshipping his beautiful tiny daughter. *"My beautiful wee princess",* he coos over her. Soon though, he has to get the plane back to Belfast where he is wanted for rehearsals of "The Diary of Anne Frank" at the Group Theatre. I stay with my delighted mother and father until I get the letter from Jimmy saying he has found us a flat, and is waiting impatiently for us to be together again. At last, we are going to be a family in one place, and, as an added bonus, Jimmy has been given the opportunity he's always wanted. He is now the director of The Ulster Group Theatre in Belfast. However, his controversial resignation over a new play

"Over the Bridge" soon puts an end to that blessed security. Again we find ourselves accepting another challenge. Our new larger theatre company Ulster Bridge Productions is formed.

While Jimmy is setting up Ulster Bridge Productions, I'm now busy as the presenter of one of Ulster Television's first weekly afternoon programmes: "Women Only." This is loosely based on the familiar radio formula of "Woman's Hour", with items on Home and Children, Cooking and Fashion. The fashion slot is just once a month, and I have complete freedom to choose the month's fashion theme; write the script; choose the models for the programme, as well as the garments from Belfast's various department stores, and to my delight, from a couple of the most expensive designer boutiques. It's a wonderful job, and I love the lifestyle it gives me, which includes the pick of the clothes, the hairdressers and free facials at Elizabeth Arden's salon at Robinson Cleaver's, whose Spring and Autumn shows are now mine to present. This results in presenting fashion shows all over the six counties. Every small shop wants to have the presenter of "Women Only" to co-ordinate and present their show. To my shame I have some very flash writing paper printed with my name inches high and a quote from one of the local newspapers: "*Ulster's most glamorous presenter*"... Writing this at eighty-seven I look back and chuckle, especially as unbeknown to the media the birth of our second baby is imminent.

Adam makes his presence known and then obviously changes his mind. The doctor has been and gone. I am lying in our bed on the fourth floor of our home in this once-elegant late-Georgian terrace in Belfast, waiting for his final late entrance. Meanwhile on the ground floor, rehearsals are progressing for the first night of "Over the Bridge" a challenging new play directed by James Ellis, the father of this indecisive baby. Ulster Bridge Productions uses the two unfurnished ground floor rooms for rehearsals, while our flat takes up the two top floors. It's working out rather well. I have a constant flow of actors coming up to check on the progress of *my* production - sitting on the bed, eating *my* grapes, while Jimmy is getting on with the fast-approaching birth of *his* production - in four days' time. The cast is also acting as baby sitters for Amanda-Jane, now two and a half years old, who is fascinated by Dad's rehearsals as well as the promise of a new brother or sister. She's busy keeping an eye on both, clambering up all the stairs to be with Mummy, endlessly asking when the new baby is coming.

In the relative peace and quiet at the very end of the evening, after nearly two days of false alarms, the doctor is called back, and an exhausted Beth hugs this new little addition to the Ellis family, hungrily sucking away at his first feed. I immediately recognise the same family features. Like Amanda he is eight and a half pounds with the same beautiful shaped head, but without her masses of dark hair. This is Adam James, our first-born son whose young life is to be ended twenty-eight years later by another young Irishman, but here I am in 1960 full of milky-ness and mothering, having just given birth.

"Over The Bridge", set in the famous Belfast shipyards, is written by Sam Thompson, a former shipyard worker himself. His dialogue shines with the intensity and authenticity gleaned from those shipyards. This is a challenge Jimmy is relishing. How excited he is, coming home to Mount Charles with Sam, along with Henry Lynch-Robinson the architect, and his cousin Ken Jamison, of the Arts Council, (all to be part of Ulster Bridge Productions) passionately discussing their plans. This has already had so much contentious publicity, especially with Jimmy resigning from his directorship at the Ulster Group Theatre. He constantly insists on the artistic worth of Sam's play, publically disagreeing with his superiors, particularly that of the principal Unionist Councillor on the board. They are horrified that the play dares to deal with the historical, religious sectarianism in the shipyards, which has occasionally even led to violence. They want to ban it, using the excuse that it is bound to offend the sensibilities of all sections of the audience and cause further disruption in Belfast. As a result Belfast and the six counties are longing to see this play that a young twenty-nine year old director has defiantly decided will be seen.

The Empire Theatre is smaller than Belfast's Opera House, but is an exquisite early Victorian horseshoe theatre; all gilded plasterwork and crimson plush seating, originally used mainly for Variety. Tragically it was destroyed a couple of years later to make way for Littlewoods, in the early sixties.

The first night is bound to be an enormous success, and obviously I am determined to be there. Still breastfeeding Adam every four hours, I know that I'll have to be home soon after the show. (How silly can you be?) It's a first night of great importance. Jimmy is both directing, and acting in it. It is an Irish play written by a volatile Ulsterman, and performed by a very large cast of equally volatile Ulster actors. Actors all over the world are passionately and obsessively possessive about their first nights, and, surely there are no other actors who can outdistance the Irish in exploiting this event to the uttermost. After a most successful performance, I am sitting on a stool by the bar in my glamorous first night dress, my breasts oozing milk and aching to be relieved by a small mouth, whose owner is by this time terrifying the babysitter by screaming the house down. Thankfully I have company to distract me: an attractive curly-haired young friend of someone in the cast. He is flattering me mightily by saying with such charm: "Ah - so you're the beautiful wife that Jimmy keeps hidden at home." In spite of the oozing milk, I immediately feel like some exotic Eastern princess. Eventually himself appears and a taxi is called. We are soon home in bed together with baby Adam, happily gulping away.

I continue presenting "Women Only" just

two weeks after Adam's birth, and this leads to even more requests from all over the six counties to present their fashion shows. I will be away from home more than before, and realise we need a live-in mother's help. This is where Sheelagh from Co. Londonderry joins the family. She's a lively wee country girl of around sixteen who has never lived in a big city, but has already been earning her living working on a farm in the Derry countryside. When I ask if she feels that two small children might be too much for her she replies airily, "Ach now Mussis Ellis, haven't I already bin lookin' after four kids, three dozen hans, an' a coupla pags - two wee babes are nothin", in her broad country brogue. I'm captivated. She's very pretty, very hard working and a total blessing to us. Like many young country girls brought up in large families she has a natural gift for nursing babies. Sometimes after bath time I watch her first with Adam, and later on with Hugo, on her lap, turned over on their tummies. One hand softly pats and strokes their back, while her other holds a comic or magazine, which absorbs her as she gently sways the baby back and forth on her knees. I watch and wonder how many years she's been practising this art of loving baby-care.

8

DUBLIN-ORSON WELLES-BIRTH OF HUGO

After selling out all performances in Belfast, "Over the Bridge" is booked for a season in Dublin, playing to capacity houses at the very large Olympia Theatre. Jimmy suggests we all come down for the last week. He and a few of the cast are staying at The Dolphin a very old established hotel, popular during the racing season with trainers and owners, including the current Ali Khan. Knowing nothing about racing, I have no idea what sort of place to expect. Sheelagh and I set off with the two children, plus all the baby paraphernalia needed for the week. We are to be chaperoned on our journey by a sports journalist friend of Jimmy's, who is travelling to Dublin to report some big sporting event. I think he finds the duties of family friend quite daunting: helping with two small children, a teenage Nanny, and especially me, wearing my large hat and elegant dress, flaunting my television and fashion-show image. We eventually become great friends. The toddlers behave perfectly, and Sheelagh has a great time giggling and flirting with him.

Once at the hotel I instantly know we are going to be spoiled rotten. The staff welcomes us with such warmth. They have obviously been members of the hotel for many years, and the atmosphere is like staying in one of Ireland's old country houses, staffed by loyal retainers who have spent a lifetime with the family. The children are adored and fussed over, and Sheelagh is immediately invited to share their staff pantry upstairs to warm up Adam's bottle, or make any snacks for Amanda and herself, at any time of night or day. They make our stay there a joy, and I'm delighted that I chose to wear my big hat and presenter outfit, as the girls admit they are all devoted to "Women

Only" – and me.

One of the most hilarious stories of the week takes place at a late-night restaurant by the famous Liffey River, which flows through the city. "Over the Bridge" - from Northern Ireland, coincides with a production by a very popular star of theatre and film. He began his career as a young man in Dublin: the globally iconic Orson Welles. He is starring with his Shakespearean company in "Chimes at Midnight". Ironically we discover that the popularity of one of Dublin's favourites is suffering from the extraordinary success of Sam's play about Belfast's shipyards. After the last night of the show when Jimmy, the author Sam Thompson, our sporting journalist and myself decide to eat at a popular waterfront restaurant, we discover that Orson is at the head of a large table on the opposite side of the room surrounded by his company of actors. Sam is like a small boy in the presence of his hero; the man he has idolized since "Citizen Kane". While we are all eating and drinking and talking, he slips over to Orson to ask for his autograph and tell him about his admiration. Apparently he is ordered away by the great man, telling him not to interrupt a private dinner. Sam comes back crestfallen, explaining: "I only wanted to tell him how he's been my idol since school days."

That should have been the end of the story, but somehow Ireland and the Irish have a talent for explosive situations. Sam goes back to apologise and explain. Before we know what's happening, Orson, a powerful figure of a man is on his feet grabbing Sam by the scruff of the neck, and the other actors are on their feet ready for a fight. Jimmy tries to reason with Welles, who is by this time shouting derogatory remarks about "*The Black North*". Amazingly he lifts Jimmy in the air. I am incandescent with fury, and march over to the scuffle, calling Orson "*a great bull*", and order him to "*stop fighting at once!*" He immediately makes snide remarks about pretty redheads coming to defend their men folk. Chairs are thrown about, and the management takes over. We all sit down at our table, while the cast of

"Chimes at Midnight" grandly sweeps out. I imagine that demon drink might have had something to do with igniting the whole affair, as well as the old traditional North v. South antagonism. It was certainly a memorable evening, and looking back - very funny.

As a postscript - and to give Orson the full credit he deserves, he accepts his first night invitation for the play's debut in London's West End. We give each other a small nod of recognition. Sadly, although the play has been sold out on tour in Scotland and the North of England, the more sophisticated London audiences are definitely not ready for a play in broad Ulster accents about sectarianism in Belfast shipyards. Our visit to London's West End is a short one.

Returning to Belfast, we start busily rehearsing the next season of plays at The Empire. Our contract at the theatre comes to an end in the spring after a very successful "Cinderella" pantomime at Christmas and the New Year. We also realise our third baby is due in a few months.

Hugo is born in July, again at home in our lovely attic bedroom. While the midwife is encouraging me to push and breathe, Jimmy takes Adam and Amanda to play in the sandpit in the Mount Charles garden. Running back up the many stairs they hear me moaning and wailing loudly as the baby is being born. Wide-eyed and worried they want to know what's the matter with Mummy. Jimmy's reply is brilliant: "She's teaching the baby how to cry." They're in through the door as soon as they hear their baby brother imitating Mummy's caterwauling; clambering on to the bed wanting to see baby Hugo in my arms; kissing and touching him, each pleading to hold him. Now we are five, quite a handful and a big responsibility for the breadwinner.

Almost immediately afterwards Jimmy's away to London to chase work. I feel very alone and deserted high on the fourth floor of Mount Charles, but remind myself that I'll soon be up and about with a busy and exciting season of autumn fashion shows in Belfast and all over the six counties.

Once the season is over however, I'm sadly no longer earning any money - not enough to pay the bills. I know I can't rely on Jimmy to send me any, as he's probably broke himself. He also has this wonderful philosophy that if you spend more than you earn, it encourages you to earn more in the future. He has no permanent address in London: staying a couple of nights here and there with friends, so I have no idea how to reach him. I must think of some way to pay the bills. I decide to run my own modelling school. I can use the trained girls, when the spring season comes along.

There are too many applicants, and I know that there are some I'm not going to be able to use on the catwalk, so alongside this I advertise "The Beth Ellis Charm School." They will virtually have the same training, but with no promise of jobs. I no longer have Sheelagh, and am now looking after the housework and the children by myself. I give them their tea around five, bath and get them to bed. Then I put on my other face, ready for the students arriving downstairs in the rooms prepared for the classes. These are rooms that had also been our rehearsal rooms. Once the classes are over I settle down to the children's washing. No disposable nappies, no washing machine. Terry towelling has to be wrung out with an iron grip, and then hung out on a drying rack heated from a couple of electric filaments in the base. After this, I collapse and sleep like a log, knowing that I can pay the household bills. The time on my own seems to be never-ending, but six months later comes the wonderful telephone call from London: "All right darling you can start to buy the Christmas presents. I've landed a part in a BBC Television series about a team of police based in Liverpool, and I'm to be one of the team who'll be going all through the series - if it's a success!"

Ohh! Now I can relax. We can have a family Christmas with presents and a tree, and turkey and mince pies at home in Mount Charles; the happiest of times together. It also proves to be our last time as family in Belfast.

For the next few months, alarming chickens are coming home to roost; Jimmy's past generosity, as the artistic director of Ulster Bridge Productions is proving to be problematic. Equipment that had been bought for the production has apparently never been paid for, and creditors are becoming impatient. There is also some controversy about the man in charge of all the company's finances, which I know nothing about. He is no longer living in Northern Ireland. There are too many worrying phone calls and threatening visits from creditors, constantly banging on the front door. Everyone advises me to pack up our home, pay the last month's rent and head for London. Jimmy's mother is delighted to have her grandchildren to care for while I am away.

I travel down the new M1, the first motorway to be built, in my second-hand Austin A40, having crossed over from Belfast on the ferry to Liverpool. It's a long drive but I am so excited at the prospect of meeting up with my new television star husband at the

Television Centre that the miles seem to get eaten up in eager anticipation of walking into the studios and announcing my triumphant arrival.

In the large, round, marble-floored foyer, I'm directed to The Green Room to find the "Z Cars" cast all sitting around, waiting for their calls. Jimmy sees me and, disentangling himself swiftly from the actress next to him, comes over and greets me with his usual enthusiasm, taking me to his dressing room. I find a woman's toilet things lying around, and her underwear drying over the edge of the bath. I stare at this picture of casual intimacy between two people. This is the repeat of a previous blip in our marriage, with an actress in "Over the Bridge" - which is now forgiven. This time proves to be worse. They are living together. It looks as if I shall have to find somewhere temporary for myself in Notting Hill, while continuing to look for a family home that we can bring the children to. At least I know they are being loved and spoiled with their grandparents in Belfast. I don't know anyone in Notting Hill, but eventually find myself a bed-sit, with one of those beds that fold down from the wall, that can be rented by the week. Somehow I need to concentrate on the daily house hunting. The priority now is to find us all a home and hope Jimmy will come to his senses. In the meantime family comes first, and as yet I haven't stopped loving him.

(It's the third blip a few years later, this time with a romantic folk-singer, when I decide to call it a day). It has been a bumpy ride, sometimes with tempestuous rows, more often with lots of fun and laughter and genuine love, but finally I think it's the hurt and lack of trust and loneliness that proves too much for me.

For now we need to be as close to the BBC Television Centre as possible, so I restrict my search to within a few miles of Shepherd's Bush. In the early 1960s, there seem to be as many To Let boards outside houses as there are now in 2015. Most families are content to rent a property, rather than buy one. Again today the cost of owning a property is so prohibitive; the majority of the population is resigned to renting. Driving slowly around the streets of Notting Hill and Holland Park, I scribble down the details of any likely properties that catch my eye. A garden maisonette on the main Holland Park Avenue eventually becomes the one and only contender. It has everything we are looking for: fifteen minutes from the television centre, a large back garden for the children, and within walking distance of one of London's prettiest parks.

This is Holland Park, with its peacocks and squirrels and rabbits and beautiful historic Holland House, with the ornate Georgian orangery, and open-air theatre: yes everything. The children love their new home, and in spite of the many traumas in our lives, No 16 is home for the next twenty years, by which time, Amanda has flown the nest, and both the boys have finished school.

Around this time our landlord decides to sell the property. I am not expecting this, but as he gives me the opportunity, as a sitting tenant, I am able to buy it at a large discount. I realise it's far too large for me to maintain, especially when I am away on tour for weeks at a time. Leaving this beautiful but ageing Art Nouveau house that's been home for so long is going to be hard. However, I start exploring possibilities with the local estate agents, and discover a newly refurbished two bed-roomed garden flat, further into The Village, near the Portobello Road. This is a complete contrast from Holland Park, as everything is very modern and minimalist, with plain white walls and two enormous sliding picture windows stretching from floor to ceiling, bringing the pretty walled garden right into the flat. I fall in love with it immediately, and once having successfully sold Holland Park, it is well within my budget.

Soon after settling in I get a visit from the young minister of our local Anglican church. Asking him in, I listen with increasing interest to his plans. He has a vision to start a ministry, with a small group of young people focusing on the creative arts, using drama and music in particular, in the church services. To my surprise he tells me that

Adam is already a member of the congregation, and naturally, I am also very welcome. I find myself increasingly drawn to this tall, bespectacled, charismatic young preacher with these exhilarating ideas, and I vaguely promise to come along one Sunday. Before he leaves, he also admits that he knows Adam is currently going through a tough time. I explain that, for now, Adam is sharing a house with four other young men, who like him, have all been residents at The Richmond Fellowship half-way house in St Charles Square. This is part of a wonderful organisation for the rehabilitation of young people who have all suffered varying attacks of depression in their teens. Following these carefully monitored weeks, they are then able to offer them accommodation in a shared house. Very sensitively, he offers any support he can give me, and tentatively suggests that he could be a surrogate father to Adam while I'm away touring. I'm so grateful for this offer; I just want to hug him. I can never guess how significant my first meeting with Rev Bruce Collins, this newly ordained, committed young Anglican priest, will prove to be one day in the future, when my life is changed forever....

9

'THE CHOICE' - 1988

Adam's murder that August in 1988 attracts wide media coverage. The press and television are covering it daily. This was the son of one of the BBC's most popular actors. Notting Hill is the home of many others in the media. My phone rings constantly. Immense waves of care and support are holding me together. Among these calls is one from a theatre director I had loved working with in the good times, at Salisbury. He has given me some wonderful parts to create. We'd created them together: Mum in "Cider with Rosie" and Stella in "Death of a Salesman". Both are strong survivor mothers. Now he's Artistic Director at Leatherhead's Thorndike Theatre:

"Beth I've heard the news. It's dreadful. Are you working? If not, I think you should be, and I have a part I'd like you to play: Dorcas, the Postmistress in "Candleford".

Suddenly I'm in tears: "Thank you Roger. This is the kindest thing that anyone has done for me right now."

"Beth, I'm not doing this for any other reason, but you are so right for this part."

"Right! Let me have the script. When do we start?"

There are loads of lines to learn. I force myself to concentrate. I am working with a very large cast who all know the situation. They rally around me, guiding me gently through the complications of working in ensemble. Suddenly I don't know my right from my left. I am muddled and confused. Travelling home after the show in the dark is another challenge. Fear takes over. This is new. I was never fearful before. Now I feel naked and vulnerable. A lone man in the compartment, or following behind me on the pavement immediately sends me into a state of panic. *Shall I stop and turn round to see who he is, or force myself to stay calm. Don't start walking any quicker. Slow down. Let him go past.*

An enormous terror of violence possesses me. Home is my only security. Everyone assures me this is completely normal. Normal? I am not feeling normal at all.

During this time Adam's ashes are to be buried in the grounds of St John's, where the funeral has been. Where the two boys carried the candles as children. I am here with the family again, coming home early from rehearsals. We stand in a silent semi-circle. Jimmy holds a little white rectangular box. Bruce ministers. The spot is between two sapling cherry trees, exactly eight of my foot prints to the middle. The careful measuring is so that later on I can plant some small tree right there. Watching Jimmy placing all that's left of Adam into that little hole, the rest of us silently witnessing this pathetic scene, gives me a sense of hopelessness, of total unreality. (How could I know that twenty-three years later, Hugo, our remaining son will be joining his brother at that same spot, eight footprints between the now grown cherry trees?)

After the short service everyone else agrees to eat together at one of the local restaurants. I don't join them, feeling constantly tired. Living exhausts me. I long to sleep forever.

"Candleford" has been the perfect answer for those first weeks, filling my empty days and nights with a purpose. There's an infectious feel-good happiness about it. Each evening the play ends with some village folk dancing, bringing the audience up onto the stage to join in. It's exactly the right play at the right time, and being Dorcas is a joy.

Now there is other work to be done. Grieving has been put on hold until after the play. Now books keep appearing from helpful friends. I read them all. Then I am introduced to Alex. Her consulting room is close by. Can she help me through this phase of grief? Her counselling room is an oasis of uncluttered calm. Alex loves white. White walls, white tulips, in a white vase. The first few weeks I sit sobbing my heart out as my eyes are drawn to the fireplace, empty but for a single small white marble image of a mother holding her child in her arms. Grief overwhelms me. Again I'm in torrents of tears. I know I will never hold Adam again. Alex encourages me to weep, sitting in silence, waiting until I'm able to speak. A solid relationship of trust, close affection and a new understanding of who and what we are to each other builds over those invaluable weeks. Maybe I can find her again one day.

Bruce Collins from St Peter's also comes to see me regularly at home. He tells me how Adam was always asking if they could pray for us, his non-believing family. He talks of forgiveness and letting go. "Adam is safe now. He's with Jesus in His Kingdom with no more pain or suffering."

Cynical disbelief from me: "Oh Bruce. How can you talk of God as a God of Love when he allowed such violence to my gentle Adam who was devoted to Him?" My first Bible class ensues - back to Genesis and into The Garden of Eden.

"God never wanted Evil to enter His World. All He asked of us was to accept His Will and obey. Man was disobedient to His one request, resulting in The Fall and Evil. Adam sitting, fishing on the towpath was being watched. Evil was stalking him there. An evening's cash was the principal focus." (Cash? Adam had £1. 20p!) "Now Beth, how are you going to respond to Adam's death? _You must make a choice"._ Why is there such urgency in his voice?

Another time, "Let's pray Beth." Obediently, I bend my head, and examine the carpet. Does he expect me to say anything out loud? I don't know how, or what to say, and so I wait. He prays, and then breaks off suddenly, "I'm going to leave you alone now. Please kneel down and verbally release Adam to Jesus' care." Quietly he adds, "Ask Him to come in and take care of your life." I take Bruce to the door, watching him take the padlock from the back wheel of his bike; bicycle clips from his jacket pocket are snapped first on one leg and then the other. He cycles off down the road.

I think of his words. "*You must make the choice.*" There was that urgency in his voice. Kneeling by my sofa, I repeat his words, "Dear Jesus, I release Adam into Your care, and...please will You now also come and take over my life. Amen." No sound of angels, no blinding light, just an atmosphere of gentleness and peace all around. Touched with Love and Comfort. I feel my hair, to reassure myself: it's still dry. Strange...it felt as if something cool was dripping on my head and shoulders. Whatever - - - I know something very important has happened.

Gradually the image of my fourteen-year old self at school praying the Damascus prayer at my bedroom window comes to the surface and how Miss Mitchell made the story of Saul's journey on the Damascus Road come alive to me. That small seed sown all those years ago was now being watered.

Bruce never suggests that any of us go to church. Not even at that last visit when he asks me to hand my life over and I feel the powerful Presence of Jesus... Over the weeks I get a strong sense I need to go to St

Peter's, the church where Adam worshipped. Tentatively I suggest to Hugo that perhaps we should go. "Just one Sunday Hugo as a gesture of gratitude to Bruce for all his care to us." We make this momentous decision. We are going to church. No one warns me I am going to meet God Himself, along with Jesus and the Holy Spirit!

The first thing that strikes me is the number of young people there. Where are all the elderly with their solemn faces, wearing their best suits and hats and gloves? These young people are all in tee shirts and jeans. A music group is playing, with keyboard, drums, clarinet, guitar and violin. All of them are young too. I watch a beautiful girl who seems to be singing solo and leading the group. Small and slight, with long dark hair, in jeans and tee shirt with closed eyes, she seems engrossed in the words she is singing. Her arms are lifted to the heavens and she looks like an angel praising the God I long to know. The rows in front of us are filled with young men around the age of Adam and Hugo. They are all singing their hearts out, stretching their arms above them. Tears start streaming. Adam has been here; lifting his arms to the Jesus he knew and loved, and singing these same words:

*Jesus we enthrone You, we proclaim You
our King
Standing here, in the midst of us, we lift
You up in our praise
And as we worship, we build a throne;
Come Lord Jesus and take Your place.*

Again I am in floods of tears... I long to lift my arms as well but feel too silly. One song after another seems to be to be speaking right into my heart:

*Be still for the power of the Lord is
moving in this place
He comes to cleanse and heal, to minister
His grace.
No work too hard for Him, in faith receive
from Him,
Be still for the power of the Lord is
moving in this place.*

What sort of songs are these? This is like no other service I've ever known. Still tearful, with Hugo's arm trying to comfort me, I speak to Bruce after the service, "Bruce what's happening to me? Why am I being reduced to tears all the time?"

He is looking slightly amused! "I think perhaps the Holy Spirit is softening your heart Beth. Lifting the scales from your eyes." The whole morning is a revelation. I begin going more and more and telling all my theatre friends about this wonderful 'New Life' I've suddenly found at the grand old age of sixty. Most of them think I've gone temporarily bonkers and hope that I'll soon become normal again.

"She's still only just surviving from the trauma of loss; give her a bit of time." And to be fair to them the early days of missing Adam are still full of pain. There are young men I see who look like him, walk like him. I hear music that reminds me of him. He was such a music lover: "Ma I've bought you this CD. You must listen to it. Let's listen to it now." Bruch's violin Concerto is one example...those yearning strings still pull at my heart. Life begins to get more and more involved with this strange community that revolves around St Peter's. Despite having lived in London's eclectic Notting Hill for over thirty years I realise I've never really been part of everyday local life. Actually I've never really been interested in anyone's lives outside the world of entertainment. A whole new stratum of local life is being opened up to me - and it doesn't always impress me.

"Would you say you have a critical spirit Beth?" I look at him amazed. 'Well of course Bruce, it's necessary for an artist to be critical, to try and produce the nearest thing to perfection!"

"Well Beth, beware. You might find you are on the receiving end sometimes." This is Lesson Two. He sees how critical I am of people and places and many other things.

10

ISRAEL – 1988

At the end of November that same year Amanda and I fly away together for a short holiday. All the family agree that I need to go away for a complete change and rest. We choose Israel because increasingly the Holy Land is becoming important in my new life. I want to see Nazareth, the Sea of Galilee, Capernaum, Bethlehem and naturally Jerusalem itself. Our small Jewish family-run hotel, just south of the city is on the road that leads to Bethlehem and within easy walking distance to the old City gates.

There's a spectacular rooftop view of the city from our bedroom window, with the Golden Dome of the Rock glinting in the sun as its centrepiece. The weather is uncharacteristically dry and mild for the time of the year, with blue skies and brilliant sunshine and the temperature is perfect for wandering around sightseeing. Apart from the city itself with its fascinating blend of Arab, Jew, Catholic, Ethiopian and Protestant all laying claim to the various Biblical sites, there are constant reminders of Adam for us. I keep seeing references to 'Adam - the man made in the image of God.' And each time I am overwhelmed with a renewed sense of loss....

We take those essential bus trips to all the memorable Biblical places and everywhere we seem to be blessed with little events of great joy. Some joyously ardent Spanish pilgrims who are sailing with us across the Sea of Galilee insist on showing us their photographs of home and families. On approaching Tiberius they start singing, and their voices lift and carry across those calm waters in exuberant praise. They are a real blessing to all of us in the boat.

Another time, while sitting halfway up the Mount of Olives talking and reminiscing about Adam, and also thinking about Jesus on that final evening in the Garden of Gethsemane, I burst into floods of tears again. If this is all part of the grieving process, I cannot think of a better location to have chosen. It's also the time of the Jewish festival of Hanukkah, and in Herod's great temple at Hebron we watch some religious celebration - with a class of young male Jewish students. One of them keeps glancing over at Amanda and me. He is wearing a long clerical-type robe and the small Jewish skullcap, and glasses. To my heightened imagination this young Jewish student is the physical twin-image of my Adam. His face and those sideways glances at us remain with me for days. After the first week of exploring Biblical Israel, we fly to the modern tourist resort of Eilat, and in one of the many luxurious hotels, we soak up the sun and the sea and the abundant Middle Eastern food, before flying back to the grey skies of London to accept the fact that I still live in Notting Hill and that Adam does not.

In the New Year, life continues as usual. I return to the A.A. meetings that I started about six weeks before Adam's death after I was arrested for drinking and driving, when celebrating my sixtieth birthday far too hilariously with theatre friends. (Driving back from Hampstead in the early hours, already half-way home to Notting Hill, I mysteriously black- out and come to having driven into the back of a parked car. The police are swiftly on the case, and leaving my now defunct car, drive me back to Hampstead police station, to be charged and sent home in a taxi. In the morning, apart from a gigantic hangover, I also feel such guilt and shame, that my first impulse is to ring an old friend who is very involved with Alcoholics Anonymous. She immediately invites me to go with her that evening for my first eye-opening meeting. My daughter's reply is unsympathetic: "Oh honestly Mummy, you may be the youngest sixty year old we know, but you sometimes behave like a six year old") I have been going to meetings regularly ever since, and receive such sympathetic support, especially when Adam's murder is announced. Looking back, I am convinced that this foolish accident in the car is my first wake-up call – the first Damascus Road experience. All through the traumatic events that follow, including the invitation at the undertakers to take a wee sip of Dutch courage, I miraculously stay without needing any alcohol at all.

11

THE NEXT STEP

I persevere with this church business and am invited to something called House Groups. Here I meet many more Notting Hill residents who all believe in God and go to St Peter's. I still feel I don't belong. Thankfully, in the Spring I'm asked to go back to Cheltenham's Everyman Theatre to play a wonderful classic Noel Coward part in "Hayfever". How can anyone say no to playing Judith Bliss? I'd already played Myra, but this is even better. I love being back in Cheltenham, and it's especially comforting to be back with my showbiz friends. Even now in my eighties I miss them and the life I used to live. Rehearsing together - creating something unique, then preparing for performance, and the terror of first nights. Afterwards, there are the parties, and the closeness of those luvvie friendships. To have been an actor for over fifty years is a very precious gift. However after a rather triumphant run at The Everyman I am resigned to going home to Notting Hill and trying to fit in with all my new friends at St Peter's. The next step is still to come. As I ask all my naive questions at these house groups, the subject of Bible colleges is mentioned.

"Who goes? What sort of people?" I ask, "Can I go for instance at my age - over sixty now?" Someone talks about a woman who on her retirement at sixty signed up to train for a missionary organisation called Youth With A Mission and now, five years later she is continuing to sail around the world on one of their Mercy Ships as their resident Evangelist. I love the idea of this. It sounds rather more adventurous than just staying in London and going to house groups and church on Sundays. I am given the present of a book from one of my new church friends.

"Living on the Devil's Doorstep" is the exciting title of this book, written by one of the early leaders of Youth with a Mission (YWAM). It is about his experiences of setting up a mission community in Amsterdam. At first they live on a houseboat, and later they move into the infamous red light district. It's a fascinating story and I'm totally immersed in it, when I suddenly read the sentence "Of course it was so much easier when we lived on the Ark". I keep turning the pages over to that sentence and remember back to ten years ago, when Adam, in his late teens, has done one of his dramatic disappearing tricks and we are all worried out of our lives until I eventually receive a phone call from him.

"Hallo Mummy, I'm in Amsterdam and I've run out of money."

Surprise! Surprise! "So how are you living Adam?" I ask.

"Well I've met these Christians and...."

I sigh in exasperation. "Oh Adam you and your Christians... I suppose they're wearing orange robes, have shaved heads and keep ringing little bells." In those days my first thought was that he was caught up with some cult or other.

"No." Indignantly, "These are real Christians and they live on a boat on the canals and they say that if I help them in the kitchen preparing meals, and help to clean the loos I can live with them, but I don't have any money to travel home."

At seventeen there is no option but to get him home, so... "I'll get Daddy to send you some money. What's the address?"

"Well the boat is called 'The Ark', and there's a box number as well." As far as I'm concerned that is the end of one more Adam episode. *Until now.*

The book I am so immersed in is about these same people who had found Adam in Amsterdam ten years ago and offered to look after him, penniless as he was. I turn the book over and find an address for 'Youth with a Mission' in Harpenden. Directory enquiries have a phone number for me, so I ring Harpenden, and ask them to send me some more information. I also receive a whole lot of questionnaires to fill in, on my possible qualifications for joining one of their Discipleship Training Schools. Unwittingly I have taken the first step toward 'The Choice' and the biggest career change for my future.

I continue with all the various St Peter's activities. Bruce Collins is still leading his flock with a firm hand and one of the core members, his churchwarden, becomes my regular prayer partner and informal spiritual guide. Jean Ross-Russell is still one of my closest friends and contacts with St Peter's and Notting Hill. Bruce takes us to one of those vast Charismatic Conferences in Brighton, led by the wonderful John Wimber. This arouses in me mixed feelings of excitement, confusion and anger, particularly at the exuberance of some of the participants as they leap about. I leave before the end, escaping back to the safety and comfort of the mid-week Eucharist at St Peter's. This is mainly for the elderly ladies, for whom I make the sandwiches. Without any apparent cause I sit and weep throughout. When I tell Bruce, he says he thinks the Holy Spirit is digging deeper and releasing more hurts in me. I determine not to be put off by these strange emotions and sign up for a weekend at a YWAM location in Warwickshire called The King's Lodge. The three days' teaching is designed to be a taster for one of their Crossroads Discipleship Training Schools (CDTS) for people over thirty-five.

I tell myself that if there are any peculiar, over-exuberant persons dancing in the aisles I shall go home immediately.

When the taxi from Nuneaton station drives up to the entrance of The King's Lodge, there is a large notice board stating MISSIONARY TRAINING SCHOOL. I want to slide under the seat with embarrassment. I'm an actress, not a missionary. The imposing redbrick building is set at the end of a long tree-lined drive with large well-kept lawns in front. It had originally been a Victorian Prep. School for boys. The hall and reception smell fresh and clean and welcoming. People are registering and then being directed to the dining room for fresh coffee and homemade cookies.

The sleeping accommodation upstairs is simple and basic. There is a bed, a cupboard, a bedside unit and lamp. On the bed is a small basket filled with some homemade biscuits, small bars of chocolate and boiled sweets. It also contains a hand-painted card with my name on, very prettily decorated with flowers and a Welcome blessing. At first I think it must be a photocopy with my name added, but on closer inspection, there is no doubt that it is hand-painted: made for me alone. I feel so touched. There are quite a large number of us and we have all been thought of individually. This is my first taste of YWAM's ministry of hospitality.

By the end of the weekend I'm totally won over by the staff and speakers. All share so much of their own lives with us. Their lifestyle puzzles me. Living by faith (another mysterious phrase) with no one getting paid for all the work they do. I love their gentleness, the way they listen and never push their opinions on to us. I'm fascinated by them, and notice there are a lot of children living there too. Walking around the back of the building I find a number of cars parked. Nothing grand, just run of the mill family cars, and the children look fit and well fed, in tee shirts and jeans, just like everyone's children these days.

The weekend closes with an amazing uplifting session of singing praise and worship songs to God (and no-one dances in the aisles!). By the time I leave The King's Lodge, there is a big warm hole in my heart that needs to be filled; a deep desire to grow more like these people. The feeling stays with me as I travel back to London from Nuneaton on a totally over-crowded train. I decide to sit in a 1st Class Compartment, ready to pay the difference but no one comes to ask for my ticket. At Euston, with my new found shining honesty, I find the Guard to say I owe a fiver and he refuses to take it! That blessing given at The King's Lodge has just been attached to me and I feel like one of C S Lewis' book titles - "Surprised by Joy." The seed sown by

Bruce Collins a year ago has been watered and fed at Youth With A Mission and now it's growing. I wonder what is going to happen next.

12

AMANDA'S STORY – HUGO'S WEDDING –YWAM

Daughter Amanda is now married and living in Surrey. One memorable weekend, she comes to London on a shopping trip, and then visits me. Coincidentally it is Pentecost, the day in the early church when the disciples were all miraculously filled with the Holy Spirit. St Peter's church has a visiting speaker and his team, who are here to do a teaching session on the Gifts of the Holy Spirit, and Amanda joins us. The following is an account of her experience which Barry Kissell - our visiting speaker, later includes in a book he has written, entitled; "The King among Us"

(Learning to Minister in the Power of the Holy Spirit).

"As a child she had believed in God and at the age of ten was confirmed as a member of the Anglican Church. However in her teens she became bored, disillusioned and drifted away. It took a tragedy and a funeral to make her think deeply about God. One summer her brother was fishing on the banks of the Grand Union Canal, unaware that at that moment his life was in grave danger. A young man armed with a knife walked up to him to rob him and in the process stabbed Adam in the heart. Within a few minutes he was dead. The robber was richer by £1.20p. Adam was a committed Christian and his funeral became an occasion of great hope. Bruce Collins, a personal friend of Adam, took the service, which was attended by many theatre friends. This was the first realisation that Amanda had of God's presence. At the time she was unable to verbalise it but something extremely tangible and loving was happening. Soon after, Bruce invited her

brother Hugo to accompany him to a John Wimber conference in Edinburgh. Hugo returned a changed man. He was no longer her angry younger brother, but someone filled with love, joy, peace and a gentleness she had only seen once before in Adam. Her brother's obvious new life coupled with the funeral service, created a longing and hunger after God in Amanda. The next link in the chain was the visit of one of our teams to her brother's church, which she attended. Amanda was surprised to find the team quite normal and down to earth, and was able to relate to them easily. During the evening worship the Holy Spirit came powerfully and she asked one of the teams to pray with her. She tried so hard to receive, and waited expecting something spectacular to happen, but there seemed to be nothing, although all around her she could see others being visibly moved by their experiences. She went home filled with hope and expectation. As she was drifting off to sleep she heard a voice repeating a word a number of times 'Listen, listen'. The following day was the celebration of Pentecost and she went back to St Peter's once more. As the worship ended, people were invited to the front to receive the Lord. As she stood there she heard the voice again whisper 'Listen'. Standing perfectly still she sought to obey. Slowly, imperceptibly, she became aware of an immense calm, her arms lifted gently away from her body and rested in an attitude of praise, tears began freely and her whole being just felt full to overflowing with love, joy and an unbelievable peace. Suddenly, she felt as though she was standing in the presence of the Lord, and although her eyes were closed she felt bathed in a pool of light. The voice spoke again "Here I am, you're not alone. I have always been here, just waiting for you to ask me into your life."

At the time I am standing close behind Amanda, and finding me there she falls into my arms still sobbing. Hugo is over the moon. He and Bruce have been constantly praying for this weekend. Now we are three!

It is now nearly two years after the traumatic loss of Adam, and I decide to meet up with the woman who joined YWAM after her retirement. We meet at Notting Hill tube station and I immediately warm to this seventy year old whose enthusiasm and energy sparkle through every sentence and movement as we walk back home. When I tell her I'm contemplating following her example and enrolling in a Discipleship Training School, her advice to me is direct and to the point.

"Go to the Hawaii base, it's so beautiful and you will get all the very best speakers - they love going." Wow, I think - Hawaii. This sounds more like the sort of adventurous life I'm looking for, *and* I can learn to become a disciple in one short term! I remember a quotation from Jamie Buckingham, 'Relinquish the past and willingly venture towards a new place. Only then can the Holy Spirit have complete control.'

I so want this to happen to me, and after filling in the application forms, I sit back and review my new life. First I have to inform the family. There's an outcry from Hugo as he has just become engaged to Rachel the young violinist in the music group: I must wait until after their wedding.

"Of course Hugo, but when is it to be?" Having got a date I begin planning both events together, although I have very little chance to do much planning of their wedding, being constantly reminded that it is *their* special day, and they are perfectly capable of organising everything themselves. Hugo is still sharing my flat and he regularly reminds me that the Bible declares 'That a man will leave his father and mother and be united to his wife,' although he keeps on using the old King James version 'cleave to his wife' which has an even darker finality to it. I assure him I'm quite ready for this cleaving, but deep down in my heart I know this to be the final loving and letting go before making the next big step along the way for my own life.

The wedding is in May, and the weather is perfect: endlessly blue skies and pink cherry blossom on the trees surrounding Ladbroke Square Gardens. The guests arrive to see Rachel looking radiant in her beautiful dress, walking the few hundred yards from the house whose many children are her bridesmaids, and who are all following her. We settle into our chairs, and the music group begins to play, with the words of the first song on the overhead for all to join in. The church is packed, as the whole church family has been invited. The formal invitations are sent to family and friends, and to those from our own world of entertainment, mostly non-believers – an interesting mix.

Towards the end of the reception, which we also hold in the beautiful setting of St Peter's, I'm sitting back and relaxing after the food and wine. I'm feeling at peace because all our arrangements have gone as planned. The marriage vows have been said, the final *cleaving* in the service is over; now there are just the speeches. I am far away in my own thoughts when Hugo's words catch my attention: "To the special woman in my life, who has borne me, bathed me, schooled me, housed me, laughed with me, cried with me, shared my moments of joy and has been with me through thick and thin and never rejected me even though she has had good reason to. In short, thank you to the woman who has loved me and been the most constant example of God's Love I have come to know through Jesus in my life: my Mother. *Thank you Mother, I think your hard service is now completed, and may you enjoy your new-found freedom and long life."* The tears start, but the last two lines remind me of our *cleaving* conversations. I take heed of them and smile to myself, thinking of Bruce's words about Adam, "Let go Beth - Love and Let Go."

Unwittingly, Hugo, in his reminder to me in the speech, has given me permission to begin my new life. Now I am free.

Now I can make 'The Choice'....

I will never forget my first glimpse of Kona's Airport.

My official photo for the school Notice Board at Kona's University of the Nations. 1991

Guang Dong province - pavements are covered with every kind of merchandise.

Sharing a dormitory with numerous women in Seoul -South Korea.

Sometimes asked to give our testimonies in churches as large as West End theatres.

The internationally celebrated floating Jumbo restaurant in Hong Kong - an amazing meal.

Trying on one of their glorious traditional Korean gowns.

A young couple in their kiosk with their 'single only' infant.

Sha Tin YWCA - a novel way of bath-time for two of the team.

Manila - A constant procession of bridesmaids and tiny pages in satin suits.

Pastor Hermie's pretty wife with baby Herald in the church 'jeepney' and three of their five sons.

Our accommodation in Batangas province in the Philippines.

The Philippine people with their warmth and openness are a joy to try and serve.

The Maranatha Full Gospel church has a devoted congregation and young Pastor.

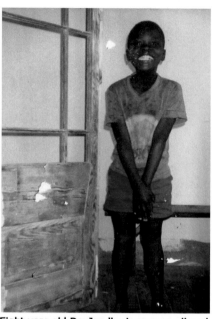

In Mozambique at 'Casa Reom' our young coach for his barefoot football team.

Eight year old DayJee 'he is very small and no one knows where his mother is.

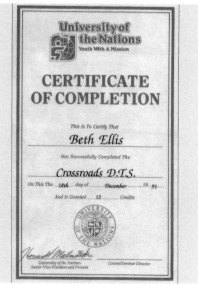

Verandahs at Casa Reom
'The House of the Good Shepherd'.

My precious certificate which I didn't really deserve.

ACT TWO

13

KONA-CDTS-OUTREACH-KOREA

The stage is set for my next adventure, leaving friends and family behind to fly away to the other side of the world. I am about to try stepping out of the boat. Will I walk on water?

My first glimpse of Kona Airport, as we taxi down the small airstrip is a sight I will never forget. Thatched palm rooftops hide behind a low wall. A big wooden gate with the sign across the top proclaims: WELCOME TO KONA. All around me are coconut palms and blue Pacific skies. A small minibus appears, and amidst cheerful hustle and bustle, our bags are packed on board, ready for the drive to our final destination. At the campus, a sign declares THE UNIVERSITY OF THE NATIONS. Here I am at last, and it's beautiful beyond all my expectations - Paradise. Palms and papaya trees set tall, among frangipani bushes, hibiscus and ripening bananas, on a slight hill overlooking the azure blue of the Pacific. The following morning I write home, "I've found the place and the people that I'd like to live with forever. Worship this morning was under an open-air pavilion. I was weeping my eyes out. Heaven, Heaven, Heaven". While reading this fulsome exaltation to my daughter years later, she remarks darkly: "And then there was 'OUTREACH'."

"Well yes," I admit indignantly, "that's the way it is when you choose to follow God." She's right though. Even after twelve inspirational weeks of teaching there is still a large question mark left in my soul. Each week we are taught a different characteristic of the God we need to know, as we set out to be one of His followers. I still struggle with it, but I love the challenge of getting to know

Him.

In the afternoons we're all expected to take part in work duties for a couple of hours. I have the fun of working in the Chancellor's office as the receptionist for the University of the Nations, and thoroughly enjoy answering the phone to callers from every corner of the world.

"This is the University of the Nations – may I help you?"

The bus stop for Kona's shopping centre is only across the road from the campus. This makes it easy for exploring the boardwalk - which leads to the many tourist shops spilling out their gloriously multi-coloured clothes and jewellery. I stop by the counter with its large bowl filled with oyster shells, and choose one to see if I can pick the pearl, and victoriously succeed. Stairs lead above the shops to a higher floor and spectacular restaurants, open to starlit skies where you can see as far as the horizon over the Pacific Ocean. I sit under the coconut palms fringing the shoreline. It's idyllic. I could happily stay forever. Every inspirational speaker gives me new aspects to think about regarding this amazing new life I have chosen, as well as filling my notebook and my Bible with copious notes. However after the twelve weeks of classes and study, comes the second challenge: OUTREACH: and 'MAKING HIM KNOWN'.

We are a school of seventy students, with numerous children. Wherever we go we split into smaller, more manageable groups. Our destinations are South Korea, China and the Philippines.

We meet together on the morning of the flight at 4.30 am! It is still dark outside, but the laughter and excitement is infectious. All of us are in pink aertex polo shirts with the YWAM logo on them, so that we can easily be spotted at the airports. All goes amazingly smoothly at Kona airport with more farewells, then over the shining Pacific and here we are at Honolulu, which is only about a 20 minute flight. We're still flaunting our pink shirts and our very impressive behaviour... "Remember last out – let everyone else off first."

Flying into Seoul, the first things I notice

are the leafless trees, bleak against grey skies. Ploughed fields have lines of snow in the frozen furrows. As we get off the plane we are met with a blast of freezing wind. The sunshine of Hawaii has been left far behind. After long queues at Visa Control and Customs, we are greeted by a large group of enthusiastic Korean YWAMers holding a banner high, with the words: 'WELCOME YWAM'.

There is now a long and dreary drive through grey concrete buildings and industrial areas. I spot endless red neon crosses over churches that light up the city skyline and glow through the greyness of this December evening. Arriving in Seoul we start to climb up a hill, passing some large beautiful houses decorated with Christmas lights, looking over the city. The house we finally stop at looks promising. When we enter I suddenly realise it is virtually unfurnished. I run upstairs, the rooms are empty - no beds! Out come the rolled up futons and the sleeping bags. Seventeen women cram into one room, mums and children in the other, with the men and boys downstairs. Those first few nights on the floor remain in my memory forever. If only I was brave enough to go to the leaders and say: "I've made a terrible mistake, I want to go home." I lie on the hard wooden floor, unable to sleep in the nylon sleeping bag that my small group leader has insisted I will need, and I try to block out all those voices thanking God for blessing us with such a lovely house... Bah! Humbug! A lot more work still needs to be done to my very spoiled actress expectations. It takes two to three days of sulking in my sleeping bag before I grumpily begin to summon up the truths of the classes I'd received week after week. I eventually dig my Bible out from the bottom of my bag, and find that morning's reading: Colossians 3... Rules for Holy Living. Set your hearts on things above... and set your minds on things above not on earthly things... I hear Him saying with a wide grin: "Oh come on Beth, see what I have in store for you." I begin to laugh, to say thank you and get up for morning prayers and worship. From that time on I venture out onto the steep snow-covered hills of Seoul, standing on platforms with the rest of our teams in church buildings as big as West End theatres, singing out songs of praise we have learned in Korean, to the delight of our enormous audiences of over two thousand young people. Not very different from being on stage really!

On the first Sunday we are up very early to visit the enormous church founded by Dr Yongi Cho. All seventy of us sing carols together on the bus journey, reminding ourselves it is very nearly Christmas. The first sight of that enormous church is awe-inspiring. One service is already in progress, so we have time to explore this impressive building, before being ushered in by waiting attendants to the front rows of the first balcony. We are overlooking a massive choir of around a hundred singers in white full-length gowns, seated behind an orchestra that could have filled London's Albert Hall. The view of the vast interior and congregation is laid out for us in all its magnitude. At one point in the service we are mentioned as honoured visitors, and we all stand up and are applauded. The service is in Korean, but we are given printed service sheets in English. Afterwards we are taken up in the lifts to the top floor, given fruit drinks and delicious Korean sweetmeats, along with a presentation on the numerous church ministries. I never knew how much the Korean Christians admire YWAM, and that many of their pastors take the Discipleship Training School. All the churches we visit welcome us enthusiastically. Gradually I begin to get our bearings, and realise that we are living a little way out of the centre of Seoul. All the houses on our hill are in a district called The United Nations village, for the many different nationalities of the UN stationed in Seoul.

A group of us have been invited to go to a special Christmas Eve service at a church, which is full of young people, probably University students. We are again invited to go onto the platform to sing the worship songs we have been practising in Korean, and we are shown so much appreciation by these lovely young people. This is a great way to spend this special evening. We travel on their rather magnificent subway system, which is a special thrill for me, as I haven't been on the tube since leaving Notting Hill in September. It seems to be an age ago, and in a totally different world. By the time we get back it is quite late. I make myself a mug of hot chocolate before falling onto my futon and, unexpectedly, sleep like a log.

The following morning I am on the Christmas Day Kitchen Crew at 7.30 am! All morning, we are kept busy organising small gifts for each other, and preparing for our Christmas Day Banquet at 6.00 pm. As usual we are all sitting round a long low table - on the floor (how I long for a chair). An empty space is kept, symbolically, for Jesus as we are celebrating His birthday...eating noodles! After the meal everyone, including the children, either sings a song or performs a sketch, which is really enchanting. I am then able to slip away to the payphone and make a reverse charge call to my precious family, celebrating their Christmas together in England with my daughter and her husband. I'll always remember his slightly sarcastic reply, when the telephonist asks him to accept a reverse-charge call from Korea! In spite of this, I am able to speak to each one of my very special family – at length!

Apart from ministry, we also have tourist-style days when we visit the National Museum and Palace and the gardens, which are covered in snow. The more delicate shrubs have their stems all cosily wrapped up in straw, which makes them look like amazing sculptures. The Palace and the Gardens are spectacular even in midwinter, especially set against a background of vast snow-capped mountains. I can only guess how heart-stopping the gardens must be in spring and summer in full bloom. Another treat is being taken to a picture postcard traditional tea-house, sitting on cushions around low tables, eating delicious sweetmeats and squidgy rice cakes, drinking fruit teas of every flavour with the dried fruit left in the tea. These days have such happy memories, but I am already becoming saddened. I have to admit to myself that perhaps I really don't have that deep-rooted Christian background and physical stamina needed to continue my life on the Mission field. Maybe now in my sixties it is all a bit too late. However this is a journey I have begun and I am determined to finish it, hopefully with some grace.

14

HONG KONG

Our next flight is to Hong Kong before we cross the border into Communist China. Many people have told me what a stunning place Hong Kong is, and I admit I've always wondered how a tiny island crowded with high-rise buildings can be stunning. But on our descent, flying low over the island I begin to understand. Nothing can describe the visual impact of this amazing city. A city of tomorrow I think, and I am reminded of J B Priestley's vision back in the thirties in his play "We Came to a City". Pencil-slim glass skyscrapers are set against a background of great jagged mountains. This is a city of white stone and glass and silvery chrome; a shimmering blue ocean in the foreground, with its many bobbing boats and Chinese junks jostling each other in the harbour.

We are driven to the YMCA Youth Village at Sha Tin, about half an hour away. This sounds promising; unlike Korea they are bound to have beds! Unfortunately this YMCA is one of the first, built in the 1920s. I guess the adjective basic is appropriate. Each cell-like room contains two iron bunk beds with a thin sliver of foam as the mattress, covering wooden planks. On the first night all my bed-clothes slide off me, as I mistakenly put their duvet thing under me to soften the planks, with my sleeping bag on top...it doesn't work. The taps only produce cold water, and the procedure is to take a large kettle across the campus to the canteen, about a five minute walk, and fill it from a tap of instant boiling water, and then carry this back for washing. I look at the cold cement floors, once painted red, the two sagging armchairs, and the row of rusting metal foldaway chairs. However we are only here for two days, and to make up for the bleak accommodation, the grounds are beautiful. I discover we are only a few yards from the ocean and the sun is shining from a cloudless blue sky. Apparently the old buildings are due to be demolished and magnificent new ones are nearly finished, painted in pale pastel pinks and misty blues. I'd love to see them now, all these many years later. That first evening, after supper in the canteen, two of the guys put together a great package deal for tomorrow, to start straight after breakfast and to end with a special dinner out. We have a free day to ourselves, and what a day it turns out to be. There are around twenty of us, and we are led by one of the team who was a high-powered executive before his YWAM life, responsible for corporate hospitality in major cities like Hong Kong. He knows exactly which of the venues he is planning to take us to. Our schedule goes something like this: 1. Bus to Sha Tin station. 2. Rail to Won Kok. 3. Walk to the famous Bird Alley. 4. Star Ferry to Hong Kong Island, (an unforgettable crossing). 5. Trek across pedestrian flyovers to the Victoria Peak tram, (taking photos all the way). 6. Tram/rail to the top of the Peak

- Wow!! And finally 7. Elevator to the lookout platform, and an even bigger Wow! where an incredible view is spread out before us, over the city and the sea to the farthest horizon. Once back down in the city itself we begin our round the island bus journey. On the way we pass Repulse Bay and the hotel, where my parents always stayed on my father's business trips to Hong Kong when we were all living in Singapore.

Stopping at Stanley Bay, we explore the famous craft market there, and afterwards I wander down to the shore alone, engrossed by the view of the whole beautiful bay as the sun is just beginning to set in vivid crimsons, over the sea on the horizon. The last treat of all is to be our dinner at an internationally known floating restaurant, way out in Aberdeen Bay. This is an enormous Chinese-style junk, rightly named Jumbo, which can only be reached by hiring one of the many sampans waiting at the harbour wall. Our sampan oarswoman is in her latter years, and she skilfully negotiates our passage between many of the floating homes jostling against each other in the bay. As we pass each one, meals are being prepared on small stoves, babies are being nursed and children are playing. Night has now fallen, and the silhouettes of the countless pencil-slim skyscrapers that surround us on the bay fade into the darkness, leaving just the lights through the glass, so that it seems as if endless curtains of stars hang from the skies and are reflected again in the dark water. It's an unforgettable scene, and rather more magical than the neon signs on the Jumbo restaurant. Our dinner is one of those amazing Chinese meals with numerous courses one after another, perfectly cooked and served with great graciousness and constantly smiling faces. Finally, warm deliciously scented flannels, passed fastidiously by tongs to each person for their sticky fingers, bring this memorable dinner to a perfect end.

After our many different stages of travel back: sampan across the dark bay, then bus to the ferry, ferry to the mainland, and the final bus to Sha Tin, we arrive home soon after eleven, blissfully happy and exhausted. I struggle, unsuccessfully, to remake my muddled upper-bunk bed in the dark, but finally manage to sleep on those dreadful wooden boards.

Our last morning in Hong Kong is taken up with a briefing on what to expect in Communist China. We also meet Edward, our Chinese interpreter who will be travelling with us. Being our final day we are also expected to do a big clean up. I feel quite indignant about this, and question it with one of my roommates who is scrubbing everything within sight. "Surely, if the YMCA has been paid for our accommodation, the cleaning is their responsibility, not ours?" She just glances up at me with a smile: "I just want to bless the place and its staff, Beth".

One more gentle lesson for me.

15

INTO COMMUNIST CHINA

Each one of us has been asked to pack some small New Testament Bibles in Chinese; with some colourful biblical pictures to give to the children we meet. The number of Bibles each of us has is within the legal limits, and we are reminded always to say that we are on a trip of cultural interest. At five the following morning we set off for the half-hour bus trip to the border. The Customs officials are brusque and unsmiling, but they wave us through without problems. One man glares at me and at my photo in my ten year old passport. "This is you?" I smile at him, nod my head, and agree. Then: "Huh - much younger!" with a look of disbelief. Of course it is, I point out; it is nearly ten years old. I've never had a customs officer make a personal comment on my appearance before, but think the most diplomatic thing is to take it as a joke and happily laugh along with him. At last we are through all the formalities of our cultural interest trip, and China awaits us... (We were warned that Korea might be the best venue of the outreach – so please remember this.)

After a bone-shaking drive our bus arrives at a very pretty lakeside holiday town. Our bus driver says he is going no further - sadly we are. Suddenly three excited Chinese guys appear with small open sided five-seater vans. I am among the first five bundled into the first van. We then set off on a hair-raising race across pot-holed lanes, just missing pedestrians, cyclists, animals and children. A terrified passenger complains: "You'd think we were competing in a race." I remember thinking; at least we are winning. Our van is way ahead of the others, but we arrive safely, shaken in every bone, to the small market town where no YWAM team has been before.

Our small hotel has a bedraggled Christmas tree outside it, next to a pile of rusty oil drums, and the main front entrance is wide open to the Reception desk, where a smiling young Chinaman greets us, with a cigarette somehow clenched between his teeth, while holding his tiny daughter dressed in her best party frock, looking immaculately clean and so beautiful. Sadly I can't say the same thing about our rooms, but I am learning to accept things as they are, and not to grumble.

Next morning we venture into the town where no YWAM team etc. etc. ... There is constant dust from the never-ending construction work from half finished buildings, and the wind from the surrounding mountains blows it relentlessly into our eyes, our hair and our clothes. Wherever we go in the town we are openly stared at, so we are constantly saying hallo to groups of children who burst into fits of giggles, and try to say 'harro' back. We discover it's a small, but fast developing and thriving market town. There's one main street with a number of small shops, and I manage to buy the local equivalent of Vim or Ajax to have a go at our rooms back at the hotel. I hear that gentle voice as I scrub away: "Bless the room and the staff Beth." Slowly but firmly I am being taught to put into practice all those words of wisdom we have been given in our classrooms.

One day, we discover there is a visiting circus in town. Edward, our translator, takes a few of us back to the caravans behind the dilapidated tent. There we meet an elderly lady, who discovers through speaking with Edward, that we are Christians. Tears well up in her eyes as she tells him they have been praying for some New Testaments, as theirs are all disintegrating. Back at the hotel, each of us hands over one of ours. These are packed into the bottom of a large chocolate box and covered by a layer of the chocolates, so that the small testaments are hidden. That evening these are given to the lady, and we receive a wonderful letter of thanks, saying she believes angels must have sent us.

My lasting memories of China are the hordes of friendly people, and their exquisitely pretty children, all so curious to see strange Westerners in their small country towns. Pavements are covered in stalls selling every kind of vegetable. Glistening mounds of mandarin oranges brim over the roadsides. I well remember those bumpy roads and the over-crammed buses, all apparently without springs. I carry away vistas of old China, with those picture-book villages set against the backdrop of hazy mountains and the relentless construction work of ugly cement and breezeblock buildings, all springing up along the main highways, striving to fall headlong into this next century, into a future of wealth and prosperity. It is a time of great transition for China. Hong Kong is to be handed back by the British, and as we now know, the Chinese are to become one of the world leaders. Finally they are given the great honour of hosting the World Olympic Games, which they perform spectacularly. All of this is unknown in 1992, but the pressure is on, and unknowingly, we are experiencing it. I remember the chill January wind that blows that building dust into our eyes and nose and clothes, and the freezing cold of our bedrooms. I try to make a hot water bottle out of a plastic lemonade bottle that becomes all misshapen. Miraculously it doesn't burst. I manage to buy a real one eventually.

As someone whose lifetime has been spent avoiding discomfort, I really have plunged into the deep end of the pool. I was not content with just going to church on Sundays, and Bible studies or prayer groups in the week. Oh no! I want to become a disciple in twelve weeks in Hawaii, and a tried and tested missionary immediately afterwards. Never have I been on a camping holiday, or slept in the open or in a sleeping bag! My closest experiences of inferior accommodation were cheap theatrical digs, mistakenly chosen from the digs list when on tour in the UK. These I would immediately change for something better, because I was assured long before the television commercial: "*Beth, you're worth it.*" Now I am learning from this life-changing experience, that what seems best to me isn't always His Choice. What am I going to learn next in the Philippines?

16

MANILA-BATANGAS PROVINCE - GRADUATION

After the bitter cold of Korea and the constant icy wind and dust on the plains of China, I now luxuriate in the heat and humidity of Manila and start to uncurl again. Here is sunshine and colour, oh so much vibrant colour! I am back to the coconut palms, the banana and papaya trees, giant banyans, and the sparkling ocean last seen in Hawaii. For two days we stay at a Catholic Hostel next to the church, which seems to have non-stop weddings with long lines of exquisite little bridesmaids in glamorous gowns, and tiny page boys dressed in white satin suits.

Eventually our large team is broken up as

usual into smaller groups, to be sent out to the various churches that have asked for our ministry. I am allocated to a team of four to the Maranatha Full Gospel Church, a couple of hours' drive further south from Manila. This tiny Pentecostal church is passionately led by an inspirational young pastor called Hermie who has a beautiful wife and five adorable sons; one still a baby in his mother's arms. He is called Herald. We think Hermie really means Harold, but he is quite definite as he tells us "Herald - like Hark the Herald Angels Sing." I think I love our outreach here in Batangas Province most of all. The people, with their warmth and openness are so easy to get close to. Their obvious delight in attending all the workshops we put on, inspires us to do our very best for them. I love the lush tropical vegetation surrounding us, which reminds me of the steamy Southern States that the playwright Tennessee Williams writes about in "The Rose Tattoo" and "A Streetcar Named Desire" that I played in so many years before. We live in what is normally the Infants School, and again we are sleeping on the floor. There are numerous electricity and water supply cuts, and once we go without either for a couple of days, existing with the light of candles and bottled water from the market, a rickshaw ride away. Of the three countries we visited, our ministry here is to prove the most fulfilling. The church is a small wooden hut, with unglazed windows, letting the air blow freely through it, and the congregation, which fills it every week, sits on simple benches. Hermie drives us out in the church jeepney (a mini-bus with open sides to let the air in), to the more distant members of the community. Sometimes he takes us to little huts high on stilts in the surrounding jungle, we lay hands on people and pray for those with cataracts or goitres; and for mothers holding terribly frail and sick babies, praying little prayers for their healing. We always leave them a coloured prayer card, and write their name on it. They hold these as if they are some precious jewel.

We're seeing so much deprivation and poverty, but receiving an abundance of warmth and hospitality, and bubbling laughter. If you asked me to choose a country to return to, it would be to these humid mosquito-ridden islands, with their pollution, the undercurrent of violence and corruption, the colourful markets and the overcrowded, gaudily painted jeepneys; with everyone hanging on for dear life. I will never forget that joyous two and a half hour service when the whole congregation welcomes us, hands outstretched to take ours, singing "We Love You With The Love Of The Lord." If I forget everything else from my first experience on the mission field, I know I will never forget the lessons I learn from these gentle people with their devotion to Jesus, and their gratitude to us.

Back in Manila, we are again scheduled to stay at the Catholic Hostel. Hermie's Mini Bus breaks down on the way from Batangas, so we arrive last. I discover that my officially delegated room with three of my closest friends, including my room-mate in Hawaii, has been invaded. I am now relegated to a bed in a large dormitory, where we all share the one lavatory and cold water basin. I lie on my bed staring at the glaring neon tube light in the ceiling. The old self-surviving spirit kicks in. Rebellion quietly takes over. I phone the beautiful hotel on Manila Bay. Yes! The Westin Plaza has a room overlooking that sparkling bay, high on the tenth floor. I go to our patient leader Bob to ask him to forgive me, and explain I need some space. I expect terrible confrontation but instead I receive his gentle reply, "Well I guess you could do with a little spoiling Beth." There is no condemnation. I want to hug him, I'm so grateful. Hooray - off to the Westin Plaza Hotel!!

A smiling uniformed porter, carrying my shabby bag escorts me from the gleaming reception lobby. As the door to my room swings open, my heart sings: 'This is Heaven.' My marble bathroom is stuffed full of bath lotions, hand and body lotions, packs of soap, sewing kit and shampoos. The lavatory works at the first tentative flush, <u>and</u> there's a telephone by it - for busy people I suppose - multi-taskers? Running the bath, I lie in the glorious warmth of the water allowing the fragrance of the bath lotion wash all the dust and fatigue from my body, and positively nurturing my soul. Next, wrapping myself in the enormous virgin white bathrobe, I lie on my enormous bed, and switch on my enormous television set. To my amazement I find myself gazing at the familiar and much-loved face of Michael Fish, one of the BBC weathermen on BBC's World Service. The London News follows. For the first twenty-four hours I luxuriate and sleep like a cat curled up on a velvet cushion. My next idle delight is people watching. Around the pool as I stretch out and sunbathe or in the one restaurant I can afford, carefully counting my last pesos. I watch them in the foyers and even in the lifts. Middle Eastern Arabs in traditional robes and gold jewellery. Glamorous uniformed air crews on stopovers, and business men from every nation in the world with their briefcases, speaking to each other endlessly of corporate accounts.

A vast waterfall tumbles into an exquisite ornamental pool on the ground floor, from a couple of stories higher, continually flowing over a transparent glass slide. I think of the power cuts in the countryside, and how we collected the precious water in pans and kettles first thing in the morning. I remember the tattered children stealing the leftovers from the café in Lipa, being chased by the owner, and how we tried to intervene by buying them bags of chips. From my balcony I watch some young urchins being chased from the hotel gardens, while playing under the water-sprinklers keeping those lawns so green. I remember that as a team we were going to visit Smokey Mountain, which is supposed to be the largest garbage heap in the world, where the poorest of the poor scrabble around in rubbish, trying to earn a few pesos, just to exist. That's where I had intended to spend my spare pesos - on them! Instead I am giving it to an International luxury hotel franchise. I'm stricken with guilt and shame. "Please forgive me Lord - you know how guilty I feel, and thank you for showing me how I've messed up. Keep on teaching me and growing me. Always remind me of that promise, printed on our classroom wall, from Paul's letter to the Philippians: 'Being confident in this that He who began a good work in you will be faithful to complete it'. (Over twenty years later, and in my late eighties, I'm still claiming that promise made by Paul two thousand years ago.)

I join the rest of the YWAM flock at the airport, and feel a slightly frosty reception from the team for deserting them. But here we are ready to fly back to Hawaii and our debriefing session, and hopefully to receive my Graduation Certificate. I know I don't deserve it – but, thankfully today I still have that precious piece of paper.

Back on the island, I fall in love with Kona all over again and make the most of our last two days, imprinting its beauty on my memory. The silver beaches and the contrast of the slate grey volcanic rocks. Purple, pink and white bougainvillea tumbles over everything. Eye-dazzling scarlet hibiscus and the coconut palms standing high, way above the luscious greenery. Everything set against the translucent blue of the Pacific Ocean. I never want to leave Kona, but now this is the time for us all to move on.

We have to say all those goodbyes and blessings, tears and hugs, and my heart confirms that my Life-changing Choice – has been just that ---- LIFE-CHANGING!

ACT THREE

17

TRAVELLING SOLO-NEW ZEALAND AND AUSTRALIA

I fly to New Zealand to continue the rest of my journey, and stay first of all with a friend from my St Peter's church family in Notting Hill. Julia had been studying medicine in London, and is now a fully qualified young doctor. Her home has a spare room, and the house overlooks the glorious Auckland Bay, with its myriad of yachts, and pleasure boats. From Auckland I take a train, called The Silver Fern that travels to Wellington to stay a few days with my New Zealand room-mate from Kona. She has a two-bed apartment right on the coast a few miles from the city. I am struck by how very English the small coastal resorts are, and we have a great time exploring this Southern end of New Zealand's North Island, and long to have the time to cross that small strip of water over to the South Island. Instead I only have one last very wet and windy day in Wellington, before flying back to Auckland, for a few more days.

Norfolk Island, in the middle of the Pacific, is my next short flight, to visit my oldest cousin Enid, whose children are now all in Australia. As we fly over Norfolk Island I am amazed to see that instead of tropical palm trees, the island seems to be covered in pine trees, which I've always associated with the Northern climes of Scotland and Scandinavia. I am blissfully ignorant of the Norfolk Pine. We drive in Enid's pick-up back to her home, set on a considerable portion of land. I see rows of banana trees covered in blue plastic bags. Enid explains that the bananas are kept in them for ripening. My cousin, already in her late seventies, is still a very active member of her community on the island, as well as a Silver Cup Winner in their Bowls Club.

To my delight she continues with her various engagements, and leaves me with the pick-up to explore the island. This is slightly daunting, as I've never driven one before. Some of the smaller roads on the island are a little tricky, and sometimes, when leading from cliff-tops they are incredibly steep, especially going from her home down to the harbour. She has been a widow for a number of years, but still has a part-time job, somehow attached to the shipping office. I ferret out the history of the British prison ships that brought our prisoners out to the island, and find the ruins of the old prisons, as well as the very beautifully maintained Colonial Governor's House, with its luxurious rooms and wrap-round verandah. There is also the fascinating history of The Mutiny on the Bounty, and I read about the many descendants of the rebelling survivors who landed here, and who can still trace their families back to that notorious tale. My visit to that small island in the South Pacific, so stuffed with British history is a very special privilege. The small airstrip, just ten minutes away from my cousin's home, is where I take my next flight to Melbourne. I am beginning to love this easy freedom of walking across small airfields on to my next plane, making travel so easy, without all the officialdom of our enormous airports. Waving goodbye to Enid, I am now off to the Australian mainland to begin visiting her five children, some of my long lost cousins. This means exploring the East Coast of Australia all the way up to the Northern Territories.

AUSTRALIA

At Melbourne though, it's another member of my home church in Notting Hill who is waving to welcome me. Helen is originally from Melbourne, and her visit home to her parents happily coincides with my trip. This is an enormous blessing; as yet again I already have a base to stay. Helen and her sister Fran guide me all around this handsome city. I often think that towns and cities are either male or female and Melbourne is for me, definitely male, so handsome, rather like London, with its solid corporate buildings. It has its pretty frilly feminine edges though, near to where Helen's home is. There we find numerous small boutiques that sell so many delicate colonial-style antique pieces, which would be snapped up in Notting Hill's Portobello Road.

Now, however, I have to meet the first of my cousins. They have organised a great party for me, and I meet two of Enid's daughters with their husbands, and all their children.

Three more cousins await me. My cousin Bill has built his own beautiful house in the style of old colonial Australia, with the verandah all round the house, on the Sunshine Coast in Queensland. It is pouring with rain when I arrive. This is where I first see countless brightly painted parakeets all coming to feed from their bird-tray on the verandah. I love the songs of so many exotic tropical birds, and Bill makes me a tape so that I can continue to hear them in the grey cold of England. The sunshine eventually comes out to play, and I enjoy myself on their long sandy beaches, with the surf rolling in as it had at Hawaii. Bill's wife Dorothy had been my Patrol leader in the Brownies and Guides, all those decades back in St Albans. We have so many laughs together over my schooldays and the memories we all share.

Now there are just two more cousins left to visit, and Bill and Dorothy drive me halfway, further up into Queensland to meet them at an extraordinary landmark called The Big Pineapple. This is a completely round building of three or four stories high and it's a perfect replica of a Pineapple. Naturally, it is promoting an enormous pineapple plantation with shops and coffee bars where we are to meet Yvonne and husband Greville. After a short family get-together, we say goodbye again to Dorothy and Bill and set off further north, to Cooloola Village.

Again I am to discover, that like so many Australians, they have bought the ground, and then built their house to their own design. This time it's Yvonne's plan, and she has chosen a wonderful futuristic design, poles apart from her brother's Colonial style. Long low eaves shade the large picture windows from the glare of the Queensland sun. The garden, only very recently planted, is already starting to flower luxuriantly, covering the sandy soil. I soon see why the soil is so sandy when they drive me out to see what they call a sand blow. In England we would refer to it as a sand dune, but this is bigger than any sand dune I have ever seen. It's like a giant mountain of sand. I've seen pictures like this of the Sahara Desert, and trying to climb up it is one foot forward and two feet back. At the summit I realise how close we are to the sea, and to an island. This is Frazer Island, and when I take a day trip out to it, again it seems to consist of sand, with the longest, whitest, sandiest beaches I have ever seen anywhere, but not a soul is seen daring to enjoy swimming in that enticing, but shark-infested sea! Each cousin's home has so much variety to show me in this vast continent. There's not enough space or time to write about everything I see and learn.

Another flight and another destination, even further north, to Cairns and the legendary Great Barrier Reef, and Equatorial forests. Cousin Robyn works at Cairns Airport, and is there in her smart uniform to meet me. As she still has a few hours to complete before she is free, she takes me to a taxi rank telling the driver to drive me into the town, and explaining where she will meet up with me later. I hand her my much-travelled bag so that now I am free to wander about and explore. The driver drops me at the end of an enormous pier with many shops, which keeps me absorbed for some time. Seeing some shady trees along the front I head for them, enjoying lying on the cool grass out of the heat of mid-day. I also find a small takeaway coffee bar and to my delight, the owner who serves me is a Londoner. He'd owned a similar bar back home, and I discover it was in Notting Hill, just a couple of blocks away from me. We greet each other like old friends, and I hear his story of how when his wife died, he sold up to come out here to join his son and grandchildren. He loves the laid-back lifestyle here, but still misses London, and admits I have made him feel homesick.

There is something about tropical heat, which makes me uncurl. I adore Cairns, and later Port Douglas, and the glorious tropical forest station of Kuranda, high above Cairns and only accessible by an incredible one-track railroad journey. This was built by the toil and at the considerable loss of hundreds of labourers back in the 1880s. Staying with Robyn and Alec and their three children is a high spot on my long journey up the East Coast of Australia. Each afternoon, after Alec gets back from work, he drives Robyn and me and their youngest boy, Tomas, out to the beach for glorious safe swimming in the shark-fence protected portion of the sea. In the deep, warm and ever wave-tossed Pacific Ocean, I am in my element - back to my own early childhood in Singapore off the Changi beach.

There's just one last stop. I have to go to Darwin. They all ask me, "Why Beth? There are no more cousins to visit".

I explain: "Once upon a time I read a book called 'We of the Never Never' a story of the early farming pioneers in the Northern Territories. It stirred my imagination, and I lived my way through all its pages." Now my curiosity needs to be satisfied. It's a very long bus journey, and I have no idea where I am going to stay, but there is bound to be a back-packer hostel. When we eventually arrive, the bus stops right outside one. So I book in – and stay one night! The following morning I set off to walk into Darwin, and after about twenty minutes I pass an eye-catching modern building with YWCA over the main door in large letters. Yes they have a room with en suite and air conditioning, and it costs slightly less than I paid at the rather moth-eaten back-packer of last night. I walk back, pick up my bag, and move into the YWCA for the rest of my stay in Darwin – and Australia.

I am on my own again, with so much to explore, and with the freedom of wandering around wearing my lightest summer clothes in that all-enveloping sultry warmth. I find the old eighteenth century prison with its trap door in the floor of the cell, and the intimidating rope noose. The friendly young receptionist at the YWCA suggests I take the ferry to a small island just off the coast. There seems to be hardly anything on it. A couple of rusty old cars that have lost their doors lie empty, still waiting for their owners. I look for the hotel I'd been told about. Then I see it. Not a soul seems to be about but there is an inviting looking swimming pool. I slip off my dress in a cubicle, having my bikini underneath and dive into the cool water. As I come to the surface my heart misses a beat. A crocodile is lying on the bottom! Instantly I pull myself onto the poolside to have another look. Yes! It is definitely there − motionless.

A guy in baggy shorts is watching me, and bursts into laughter, "It always tricks every newcomer. It's in the tiling − designed to terrify!" Deciding this must be Northern Territories' sense of humour I join in the joke.

Next day I book the coach trip to Katherine Gorge, in the land of 'The Never Never'. Our guide is a gorgeous six-foot sun-bronzed guy to die for, wearing the mandatory baggy khaki shorts and, unbelievably, a wide brimmed hat with corks dangling round the edge. Do they just do it for us tourists? The empty arid landscape we drive through is eerie and awesome. Passengers in the bus are unusually silent as we drive through this wilderness. The journey's destination, Katherine Creek, is a deep silent stretch of green water, imprisoned between two dizzyingly steep walls of rock. The canyon is called Katherine Gorge. Our wondrous guy tells us that this is the season that the crocs lie fast asleep on the bottom. It is perfectly safe for us to swim! They only attack if they think they are being molested. I wait to see if anyone is brave enough to go in. Eventually I step very gently into the water and make sure I am only floating on the very top and not splashing around at all. I do not want to wake those sleeping monsters, or come to any misunderstanding with them. The cool green water is wonderfully refreshing after the long drive, but I do not stay in long before clambering out and being helped onto safe land by our hero of the bus.

On our way back we stop for refreshments at a fairly basic café. It's more of a shack really, but we are all grateful for the cold drinks on offer. I notice a shelf of second hand paperback books for sale, and, to my surprise, find a copy of The Mission. It reminds me of Adam. So I buy it. What an odd place in the whole of Australia to come across it, but in a strange way, Darwin is like that.

The manager of the YWCA tells me there's an arrangement with the YMCA that we can use their pool. I immediately decide to take advantage of this. The building is within eyesight of ours, and the pool looks so inviting. I have no idea though what a shock it is going to prove for the male residents to suddenly find a female, in a bikini, floating around in their pool. One or two are curious enough to come and chat to me. It's fascinating to hear their stories. In particular, there are two guys from the UK - and reading between the lines, I get a sense of them attempting to escape from something or somebody, by living here in the YMCA in Darwin for months on end. Maybe they have found this 'end of the world' place somewhere to recover from some fear or sadness. I make up stories about them.

I will never forget another night, wandering back alone from Darwin's cinema, having spent the evening watching a film I hadn't seen before. There is a mysterious depth of darkness in a tropical sky, but suddenly the whole heavens are alive with sheet lightning. I've seen forked lightning before, which comes with thunder. This though is eerily silent. It fills the entire expanse of the blackness, and keeps repeating itself again and again. Standing stock-still, on an open headland totally mesmerised by this extraordinary power, I stare up at the sky with tears streaming down my cheeks. This is "Wuthering Heights" in Darwin; never to be forgotten.

My last ticket to the Island of Bali is not used. By the end of my days in Darwin, I am ready to fly back home. I have run out of energy, and money. Now all I want is to get on a plane and head for the UK and home, which feels a very different world away from Darwin at the top end of Australia.

18

HOME AGAIN: 'RE-ENTRY'

Well I've done it! I've been away for nine whole months, away from the rarefied surroundings of Notting Hill with its elegant houses and beautifully kept gardens. This is a way of life we all take for granted, but suddenly I am seeing it with different eyes and in my arrogance, judging it and all these newly found Christian friends. I tut over all the designer dresses and hats worn at a church wedding. I am shocked by hearing the popping of champagne corks, as the bottles are being opened for the guests after the service. Although I seem to remember I am quite happy to drink it! (*Oh yes - I am now considered off the danger list of alcoholic dependence.*)

The next few months I spend re-adjusting to this former life, or as the YWAM book calls it, experiencing 'Re-entry' (Making the transition from missions to life at home.) Well of course, I'm not a real missionary, probably never will be, but I have been living so closely with a group of people who are, and spending every waking hour with them, attempting to minister to deprived people in remote places on the other side of the world. Now I realise my horizons have been stretched: *Enlarge the place of your tent, stretch your tent curtains wide, do not hold back. Isa.54v2.* OK! So I have. Now I need to manage re-entry, to accept my old life without prejudice and to value people where they are. I try to remember and obey everything we've been taught in our final sessions of de-briefing: *"Above all, go home to serve your church."*

I get involved with running the weekly house groups and helping with the bookstall, joining the rotas for making the coffee, and being a Welcomer. I find I still want to learn more and more, so I join the course for

Pastoral Care and the Preaching and Teaching sessions. Eventually however, I realise I need to live my life in a different gear. The boundaries of London life, and home in Notting Hill are no longer enough. How, and especially where, is my next step to be? My months of indecision end with a call to the YWAM community at Harpenden, just twenty-five miles North of London. When I ring their personnel office, they ask me what my giftings are. I don't really understand what they mean. I explain that I've just been an actress until I was sixty, when I became a Christian. There is a pause at the end of the line, and then: "What about Hospitality"? It's my turn to pause, "Erm... Do you mean housekeeping? I've done that all my life."

YWAM Harpenden becomes my next home in the spring of 1993, as I run Hospitality House for approximately eighteen months. I want to create an atmosphere of peace and quiet, with pretty fittings and furnishings in the house for returning missionaries, and for the various speakers coming to teach at the many different classes and conferences. This vision remains with me for the entire time I am there, in spite of various difficulties. The lack of resources is one, with ancient washing machines and vacuum cleaners breaking down. Sometimes the lack of communication and misunderstandings between people from the many different cultural backgrounds cause me much hurt. I'm often in tears alone in my room, but my love for 'The Oval', and the vision for its purpose and future as laid out by its inspirational leadership, stiffens my resolve.

I will always remember the love and encouragement I am given, from so many staff and visitors. Over twenty years later, I still have many happy memories. One thing I find so difficult is to make-up the linen on the bunk beds. I remember grumbling to God, asking Him, "Why in my sixty-fifth year have You landed me with this awkward bed making?" and hearing; "It's not your bed-making skills I'm interested in Beth. I'm just trying to grow your heart for loving and serving others."... I'm still working on it! ....

During my time at Harpenden, I hear about the many different ministries that YWAM has all over the world, and that are looking for more volunteers. One morning I attend a lecture and video, showing medical work being carried out in Mozambique. There is a particularly harrowing scene of an operation in a tented clinic. A small boy has stood on a landmine, and doctors are delicately removing the shrapnel from between his legs. I start to sob, feeling so useless, having no medical skills. What use is an actress in critical situations like that? How can I be of any help? I am reassured. A short-term mission team is going out to Mozambique, to Beira an old seaport, to live and work with a bunch of street kids who have lost their families in the civil war. "Go with the team Beth, and help in their daily care. Perhaps you can do some drama with them, get alongside them. Make them feel valued."

The more I think about those children and the danger they are in from landmines left behind after the civil war, the more I become determined to start making plans to meet up with the team.

As usual they are all much younger than I am. I'm getting used to this in Youth With a Mission. Our leader will be Sally, a young nurse who also has a smattering of the Portuguese language. We attend a series of meetings, learning a little of the history of Mozambique, and being given some idea of what to expect when we get there.

The civil war began in 1977 soon after Independence from Portugal, and over one million lives were lost in the fighting, and from starvation. Many lost their limbs from the landmines. Now the war is over, but the country is still in the aftermath, with great shortages. Cities are shattered, and five million people are homeless. This includes thousands of children who have lost parents. It's a daunting project, but the young people I'm going to be travelling with lift my spirits with their enthusiasm, and the obvious compassion we share for these lost children who have nowhere but the streets to live in.

19

MIRACLE WITH MOZAMBIQUE'S STREET KIDS

A couple of months later I am in Casa Reom, translated as The House of the Good Shepherd, in the centre of Beira. War-torn, crumbling and ramshackle, but home for the next few weeks. Lying in bed with the mandatory mosquito net, I listen out for the nocturnal rustling of a little companion. Is it a mouse? It might be the giant cockroaches, but when I see that my shopping bag has acquired a small round hole in the middle of the night I know for certain that my mouse is exploring the possibility of finding 'food, glorious food'. But I have already learnt never to leave anything edible anywhere. I dread having to go out to the toilet on the verandah during the night, trying to avoid the cockroaches, or even worse, the odd rat or two; but working and playing with our boys makes up for all the other discomforts.

Around a dozen boys arrive in the mornings after their night sleeping on the streets, and use the shower that has been rigged up on the verandah. A good breakfast follows, cooked by the two Mozambican women who come in, each with a sleeping baby wrapped in a sling on their shoulders. Afterwards they all join in an enthusiastic session of loud and very joyful praise and worship songs on the verandah, attracting the attention of passers-by in the streets below. They look up in amazement at these young voices so obviously enjoying themselves. During these weeks I start to love these lost youngsters who seem so unaware of what life should be offering them. Many of them I am told are already suffering from HIV and their response to our care is overwhelming. I want to pack them all up and take them home with me.

I discover how much they have come to

love us one evening when we all gather in my bedroom, rather desperately praying for one of our young volunteers. On my way to bed earlier I find Chris gently sobbing outside my door. He has mistakenly been taking too many of the incorrect tablets for protection against malaria, and his heartbeat is racing. He is in charge of the boys' afternoon football sessions, and the extra physical activity has accelerated the condition. He is only twenty, having just completed University, and is now a student teacher. He says he feels exhausted, but too frightened to sleep: "In case I don't wake up Beth."

I do my Mum thing and call everyone together to pray for his healing. The local doctor is away on his annual furlough, and we have no idea when he is due back. The team all squeeze into my little room, gathering round Chris, and we begin to ask for his healing; for his peace of mind; for the doctor's return...for... but before we get any further, there's a quiet tap on the door. It's a group of the boys, "Please Beth can we come and pray for our Chris too - we love him very much." I pat the space on the bed next to me, "Of course, sit here." So they all snuggle up close to me, and to each other.

I start the prayers again followed by the rest of the team...Jayne, Jackie, Alan, and then - the little husky, throaty voice of eight year old Dayjee starts rattling along with great earnestness. My arm hugs him. He is very small and no one knows where his mother is. He was just picked up off the streets. Here he is, leaning against me praying away so passionately. I start to sob, gulping away, tears streaming down my face. The moment he says "amen", Constantin starts another long prayer, again in Portuguese, and then it's picked up by Jeremias. These children are little rejects - flotsam and jetsam - the African equivalent of Fagin's street urchins in Dickens' London, and here they are, praying to *Senor-* God to make Chris better. I know at that moment that *Senor* is with us - the room is filled with His love. The rest of the UK team are all in tears too.

Just then our youngest team member, seventeen year old Sarah, walks in with a saucer of cooking oil from the kitchen saying: "God has told me to anoint Chris for his healing". She kneels by his feet to anoint his head and his hands with her fingers, and in the silence, the house phone begins ringing. We pause, and wait to hear the base leader call: "Chris it's for you, the doctor's just come back and picked up our messages, go and talk to him."

Just a coincidence? …. Or do miracles still happen….?

Chris receives medication, which acts as the necessary antidote to all the incorrect pills he has taken, and he is soon back to his cheerful self again, coaching his enthusiastic, barefoot footballers.

20

LONDON AND THE 'MOUSETRAP'

Back home I have so many stories to tell about my adventures and the children at Casa Reom. Our Sunday school children at St Peter's immediately identify with these street kids, around their own age. Schemes are started in order to send money to help them. Homemade cookies appear at the end of morning services, along with a notice: "YOUR SMALL CHANGE WILL HELP SUPPORT THE WORK AMONGST THE STREET CHILDREN OF BEIRA, MOZAMBIQUE." My stories make them aware of the stark contrast between their own privileged lives in Kensington and Chelsea, and these young orphans in Africa. Their Mums and Dads in church respond so generously. We send a letter from our children with the money.

My commitment to YWAM Harpenden is now over, and I have no idea what the next step is going to be. I decide just to stay put, getting involved with life at St Peter's. Christmas isn't far away, and the Youth Group persuades me to help them with some drama performances. At the same time I'm wondering whether I might try to learn Portuguese in evening classes, in case I am meant to return to my little boys. I have a go, but soon give up. There seems to be a new way of teaching languages, where the teacher comes into class rapidly speaking away in this alien language, and shoots questions to her students, expecting them to both understand and reply. Everyone else seems to be so clever, and I am overwhelmed, putting it down to their youthful brains. I don't know how to compete with their astuteness, and slink away in shame. Oh well, perhaps I have not been called to go back after all. Patience is being called for to see what happens next.

Soon after all the Christmas festivities are

over I have an unexpected phone call from a young actor, telling me that he has been going to the auditions for the next cast of "The Mousetrap". The director has asked him whether he knows if Beth has stopped *circling the world.* I ring him, not so much for a job in "The Mousetrap", but because David and I have been good friends for many years. He asks me to come and read for the part of Mrs. Boyle, who is a magistrate in the play, and a right old battle-axe.

Suddenly I find myself back in the theatre again, without writing a single letter, or making any effort on my part at all. This seems to be another miracle, and quite clearly my next step is to start making that daily journey to a West End theatre, taking a purely secular job, instead of attempting to learn Portuguese, and returning to Mozambique. This is an unexpected about-turn on my new mid-life career change. A very different challenge....

Having spent forty years in the theatre, my life has had its fair share of unexpected happenings, but to find myself sitting in a theatre dressing room again, seems to be quite bizarre. Only a few months before I was living among the cockroaches in a ramshackle YWAM Mission House in one of the poorest countries in Africa. Now, here I am in London's West End, calmly setting out the necessary tools of my trade in Dressing Room No 1 at Saint Martin's, one of London's most famous theatres; mainly because it houses the longest-running play in the world.

My windows are open wide, letting in as much of the night air as possible in the summer heatwave we're having. I hear the hum of nearby traffic, a taxi horn and squealing brakes. There's the smell of something delicious being cooked at a nearby restaurant, teasing my taste buds. It's probably 'The Ivy' that rendezvous of theatre stars and other celebrities, which is right opposite the theatre. A montage of all my street kids in Mozambique covers my dressing-room walls, as well as all the Good Luck cards for the first night from many friends, delightedly welcoming me back. My own much-loved family also features large, with their photographs on my dressing table. Plants and flowers spill over the windowsills. It's HOME! For the last four or five years though, I've been insistent: "Please don't think of me as an actress. I used to be an actress. Now I'm in missions." Whenever I have to fill in one of those many official forms we are deluged with these days, I always put retired. This seems to make perfect sense.

It is over twenty years since I last made this journey into a London theatre every night. Not since the years at The Savoy, The Piccadilly and Duke of York theatres in the sixties and seventies. The West End has changed a lot in that time. Before, it was possible to drive myself in my own car, and find a parking place. Now that is impossible. It has to be by bus or underground. I am rudely awakened by the total disregard that travellers now seem to have for anyone but themselves; 'push in and get a seat no matter what', appears to be the general philosophy. The escalators at Tottenham Court Road are packed with every nationality. I realise that London now is a total microcosm of the world. The sleazy half-mile from the theatre to the Underground, on my way back home after the show, fills me with trepidation at first. The sex shops and film shows with their lurid titles trouble me. The disco clubs with their over-sized tattooed bouncers at the doors, and the drag queens tempting new customers: all these are worlds away from the gentle leafy suburbs of the YWAM community in polite Harpenden!

I remember the words spoken to me by one of the University of Nations leaders there, "You ought to go back to be a light in the darkness of your world Beth." It seems more scary than the rubble-strewn city streets of Mozambique last year. As I get accustomed to the jostling young though, queuing for their discos, and the lively street theatre, I realise it's mainly due to my over-active imagination. In those sweltering summer nights I stand by the traffic lights at Cambridge Circus waiting to cross, feeling the heartbeat of London's West End. Twenty years ago I would have hurried up the side streets into Soho or Covent Garden to the late night theatre clubs until the early hours, and then driven myself home in my little Hillman Imp! What sort of mad woman was I then? Perhaps it was a strange kind of grieving for my lost marriage, putting on a front - proving that I was having a wonderful time - "Me? I'm fine." Now I am content to hurry by the hot-dog stalls and hamburger vendors, merely glancing down those neon-lit side streets, wanting to get home in time for "Newsnight" and put my feet up.

One night In particular stops me in my tracks, as I hear the liquid notes of a saxophone across the street from the shadows of a building. The yearning melody of 'Stranger on the Shore' lifts me far away from the Charing Cross Road to somewhere in the deep south, to the Mississippi; to St Louis, New Orleans, the world of "A Cat on A Hot Tin Roof" and Tenessee Williams. I will treasure that sound, the lights of The Palace Theatre and the posters for "Les Miserables", the gaiety of the masses in Covent Garden and Leicester Square, and everyone wining and dining al fresco in this scorching summer. The airless city heat is comparable to a night in any African city. I remember the flower stalls in Earlham Street, a mass of eye-dazzling colour, and all those bistros and boutiques flourishing in Covent Garden.

I celebrate my sixty-seventh birthday, along with Hugo and Rachel after the show, at 'The Ivy'. It's such fun spotting the famous, as well as savouring the delicious food and impeccable service. This transpires to be my last goodbye to the bright lights of West End theatre land, but my journeying further afield is by no means over yet.

At the end of my six-month contract, I am offered the following six months, and I admit I am tempted to extend this trip beyond its sell-by date, but another interior voice is urging me to *step out again and test the waters; see what else is on offer.*

So...the contract is over. I no longer have my cosy second home in the heart of theatre land, but the memories and the essence of those six months remain indelibly captive there.

21

VARANASI AND KATHMANDU

James and I meet during my time at Harpenden. A tall lanky American in his early thirties, he had been an interior decorator before joining YWAM. While on the campus, he gives a complete make-over to a couple of the house interiors. I am very impressed, and make a mental note to keep in touch. Soon after he leaves the campus, he marries and brings his new wife, Monica, to see "The Mousetrap", visiting me in the dressing room afterwards. James' vision is to return to India where he was on outreach, several years before. His interior design jobs are a way for him to earn some cash for the journey. Sponging and rag-rolling is the current fashion trend, and is something James used in Harpenden. "Please James, come and give my new flat the same make over. I can pay him to up-date my new trendy garden cottage in the heart of Portobello Village with my savings from "The Mousetrap". This is a project that will benefit us both.

Each day we talk about his plans for the future. His vision is to live in the legendary city of Varanasi, reputed to be the oldest city in the entire world where Hindu worshippers come to be cleansed of their sins in the iconic river Ganges. During our time together, my imagination begins painting exotic pictures of India from everything he's telling me. Gradually my plans for an 'encouraging James' visit start to take shape. Soon after he finishes the wonderful job he has done for me, he flies to India, and we regularly keep in touch.

The plans he has for running a small restaurant called 'The Bread of Life' are coming together very successfully, but between the lines, I sense his disappointment. None of his missionary friends in YWAM have come out to join him. I feel desperately sad for him, and make my final decision to visit.

Soon after I celebrate my seventieth birthday. Every ten years I always make a point of planning a very special birthday treat to share with family and friends, and each one gets more extravagant. My sixtieth was my last with Adam, and which he helped me plan. My seventieth includes all the St Peter's church friends, and appropriately we take over St Peter's own restaurant in the Portobello Road, with a jazz quartet from the musicians in the worship band. Hugo plans a secret "This is Your Life" for me, based on Shakespeare's 'Seven stages of man.' It's an amazing evening, and even Jimmy is present. My eightieth is to be even more extravagant... but more about that later.

Now, I book my flight to Delhi.

It is 1998 - ten years since Adam's murder - and 'The Choice'. Finally the signpost is clearly beckoning me along 'The Way' that leads *from* Footlights and *on to* Faith.

James organises a couple of young Indian

drivers, (employed by the Delhi hotel I'm booked into) to meet me at the airport and take care of me until he arrives. They are wonderful company and drive me to Agra the following day for the mandatory visit to the Taj Mahal. The crowds and the harassing photographers at this magical site take away much of the romance that I have been expecting, especially as there is some problem with the fountains which remain empty. Instead I am fascinated, watching the groups of graceful women in their jewelled saris; giggling and laughing as their men folk take endless photos of them. I keep thinking of the photograph of our own beautiful, abandoned Princess Diana sitting alone in front of the fountains, which are dancing and shimmering behind her. Flying around the world, so often on my own, I can identify with her loneliness. However, James is arriving tomorrow and we are taking the final flight to Varanasi together.

The journey seems over far too soon. I wish we had been on one of those overcrowded Indian trains, travelling with the people, seeing the changing scenery as we cross this vast continent. James has a time limit however, and this is the best choice.

His Hindu partners in The Bread of Life have booked me into a guest house overlooking the Ganges at Assi Ghat. Our journey from the airport eventually leads us through the narrow streets of Varanasi, with our driver madly dodging cows, goats and people, bikes and rickshaws, until we arrive at 'The Ganges View.'

I can hardly believe that I have been so blessed with such an exquisite place to stay. There is nothing European about this elegantly decorated Hindu-style residence. I note the intricately painted arches over each door, and also right up the wide stairway to the verandahs. My doors open onto a roof garden with a view of an ornate temple, and the Assi Ghat, with steps into the Ganges for ritual bathing. I love the wall paintings over each of my doors and on my bedroom ceiling. I catch the hushed whisper of ceiling fans and the gently billowing muslin curtains, white against white, at the entrance to my rooms. Yes - rooms! Apart from my large bedroom and the wet room with its hot and cold water, I have a small ante-room, for receiving guests. This is formally furnished with three chairs set around a small occasional table. In the centre, a bowl of water is filled with a mass of floating petals, tiny pink blossoms, another delicate example of authentic Indian hospitality. However, the *piece de resistance* has to be the large basket filled to the brim with homemade cakes and cookies, all wrapped up in cellophane and tied with satin ribbon, topped with a Welcome Card from the Staff of The Bread of Life Bakery. All of this has been organised by Ashish, who is the owner of the bakery premises, and also James' partner in the restaurant.

My breakfast each morning is brought to me on the roof garden, overlooking the wide Ganges, facing east as the sun rises. I watch the Hindu worshippers arriving early to bathe in the 'sacred' river in order to be cleansed from sin. Pujas (small sacrifices of flower garlands and sweetmeats, and floating candles) are offered to the river, while an everlasting chant and the response crackles over the loudspeakers from the adjacent temple, with its many chattering 'holy' monkeys! 'Holy' cows render a backing of mooing from the riverbank below. I look over the parapet to see which cow is responsible, and I'm fascinated by the procession of humanity making its way down to the river's edge. Young westerners, dressed Indian-style in saris and beads, are followed by a nearly naked 'holy' man with white painted face. Saffron robes reflect the sun, as three shaven-headed priests walk in solemn meditation. Donkeys are driven up the lane, with enormous pannier baskets filled with cow dung, to be dried into bricks or fuel for winter. A line of about twenty cross-legged beggars wait patiently with bowls for their daily meal, brought to them in a small mini-bus. Over all this thronging activity it's the vivid colours, which catch my eye. The brilliance of the women's floating saris, defying their often desperate circumstances, are in colours that provide an artist's highlights against the sober beige and browns and off-whites of their men folk.

Enough of this people watching and daydreaming! I am here to encourage James, and to help wherever possible in his visionary restaurant and bakery. Currently there are around fifteen young men employed as waiters and kitchen staff. They might otherwise be unemployed or working illegally as moneychangers on the streets, or touting for trade on the riverbanks. I am here to help teach them English. They have a regular Hindi-speaking teacher, who is also a local pastor. The boys are in their late teens, and only one is a Christian, so there are to be no overt allusions to Christianity. One day I tell them the story of two brothers who work on their father's farm which one day they will inherit. The younger of the two longs to leave the hard work of the farm for the bright lights and discos of Delhi, and loses all his father's money. Later we all discuss the story, and the boys tell me they will never act like the younger son. They all identify with the elder brother, and his responsibility to the family.

Another time, having been to the gloriously elaborate Hindu wedding of Ashish, we role-play the prospective son in law being interviewed by the bride's father. Fuldev, who is playing the father, says to Narayan, "But we are a Christian family and you are a Hindu, Do you love my daughter enough to leave your faith for *ours*?"

Narayan replies: "Yes I love her." Protests of disbelief come from his classmates.

"No! No! No!" laughs Fuldev (the one Christian), this is just a game."

I learn so much more from them than they can ever realise.

Looking back from the security of my life here, in spite of our current season of austerity, the memories of Varanasi come flooding back. I travel everywhere by rickshaw and hang on grimly as we plunge into potholes and over bumps. We dodge the enormous garbage heaps in the middle of the road, and avoid the men using the makeshift urinals in the gutters. I can still picture the barefoot and beautiful children chasing chickens and mangy dogs amongst the rows of roadside barbers and traders of anything and everything under the sun. I remember the little family of a mother and her small son and daughter, as well as a baby, who live on the bank of the river in a large cardboard box. They insist on giving me their Christian tracts as a present when they notice my small cross. They proudly tell me they are Christians too. One of their tracts says 'A new start' with a picture of a butterfly. They are so beautiful in torn and dusty clothes. I feel such love for them and awful uselessness, as I leave for my next stop ... Nepal and Kathmandu....

On my last morning I am up before sunrise. The Ganga is rose pink, and soon that fiery red ball sends a solid red path across the water from one bank to the other. Young Prakesh brings me my breakfast as usual and the thieving monkeys from the temple, as well as the birds perched waiting for crumbs, are my faithful breakfast guests for the last time. Mr Shashank Singh, the ever courteous and gracious owner of The Ganges View, once his own family home, orders the taxi for me. As it slowly drives me down the main street, I find myself leaning out of the window, waving goodbye to so many people who have become my friends, as they look out from their small kiosk-type shops. James has all the boys lined up to say goodbye at The Bread of Life. I long to hug them all, but of course I cannot: "Namaste, Namaste," has to suffice.

The flight to Kathmandu is only forty minutes, and the young man next to me gives me his window seat as we fly over the Himalayas: miles of snow-capped peaks and daunting ravines below. At the airport there are so many forms to fill in and I haven't any photos for my Nepal Visa, and only Indian rupees. I completely forgot that Nepal is not India! When I am asked for seven thousand Indian rupees, I find I only have six thousand nine hundred, but am waved through. Finding the cash desk, I get some Nepalese currency, am grabbed by a taxi driver and driven to the Kathmandu Guest House.

Arriving at the main centre, I am transfixed. After the uncompromising lack of western consumerism in Varanasi, the narrow winding streets of Kathmandu are lined with gloriously seductive looking shops, their windows stocked with every consumer-driven goody that any shopaholic's soul could crave. I feel puritanical! This is tourism gone mad. We drive through the imposing gates of the Kathmandu Guest House, through a courtyard filled with flowering shrubs and trees. This is to be the centre for the rest of my stay in Nepal. This choice has been made, on the advice of a couple of American missionaries from Bangladesh, who were staying at The Ganges View, and it proves perfect. Now I just have to contact Prejwal, - who is to be my guide and companion all through the Kathmandu valley. I was given a letter of introduction to him from Arlene, a pretty blonde Californian woman staying at The Ganges View. She comes to stay at Shashank's each year, to study with her Buddhist teacher at an Ashram in Varanasi. She also encourages me to visit Nepal and meet her 'brother' Prejwal - a classical Buddhist dancer - who will look after me. She also gives me his phone number, so this is my next step.

The following morning Prejwal arrives on his motorbike at 8.30 am. I am so impressed by this handsome young man in his twenties, who gravely welcomes me to his country with such gentleness and perfect manners. He plans to spend the entire week taking me all around his beloved Kathmandu, and the valley beyond the city. He anxiously enquires whether I am used to riding pillion on a motorbike.

"Erm - well no, but thank you Prejwal - I'd love to have a go." Inwardly I'm thrilled. I want to laugh out loud, wondering how many elderly ladies in their seventies have the chance of zooming around Nepal on the pillion of a young Buddhist dancer! I feel like hugging him with joy. Naturally I don't. Apparently in her letter to him, Arlene has asked him to take me to see the hotel where he and his troupe of dancers are employed, so I swing my leg over the bike in a show of great experience, and off we go...whizzing uphill on a steep and rocky road to the Vajra.

This is the one that Arlene raves about, and it is stunning. Architecturally it is quite unique, designed and decorated in traditional Nepalese style. Prejwal explains it was originally the home of a local grandee. We climb up to the roof terrace to see the view over the whole Kathmandu Valley, still wreathed in mist. This would be an incredibly beautiful place to stay but sadly, way out of my budget. I wonder if I will ever see myself in the role of the rich old lady, instead of budget old lady. Anyway the rich old lady is most unlikely to have the adventure of being whizzed around Kathmandu on the back of the motorbike of a delightful Nepalese dancer.

Each morning Prejwal arrives on his bright red Honda with a plan mapped out for the day. I see every noteworthy temple in Kathmandu, and the valley beyond. We climb hundreds of steps to monasteries perched on topmost peaks, with Prejwal apologising, "I am so sorry to tire you Mama", as I pant and gasp for breath. We watch prayer drums being revolved round and round and hear the metallic clanging of huge gongs, and the gentle chanting of monks praying. I watch some temple ladies silently dusting all the statues and the altar, and there, amongst all the graven images stands a tall carton of Pringles! I can never forget the 'caff' in the tiny mountain village where Prejwal decides we will lunch. I deliberately call it a caff, as surely it's the equivalent of our greasy spoon. The food is delicious, but forget the hygiene! We share our small space with two monks, two dogs and two village men. I would never have dared to go in without Prejwal. Two women in Tibetan dress, which I have never seen before, are walking along the village lane in ankle-length narrow tunics, beautifully simple without embellishment. So many memories, I long to recount them all, but many have to be left out. So I quote from my journal:

"*Today is the 1st December, three weeks more and I will be back in Notting Hill, celebrating Christmas at St Peter's Church, with my precious children and grandchildren, but here I am being taken by Prejwal to the*

Monkey Temple. This is one of my favourite trips. I mount the Honda again and feel quite professional, especially as I seem to have chosen the right clothes for pillion riding with my leggings and track shoes, and my all enveloping wrap from the Portobello Road in Notting Hill. Coincidentally it's the same crimson colour worn by all the Buddhist priests over their saffron tunics. Neither Prejwal nor I have helmets, so perhaps it's not expected over here. I have said a little prayer asking God to protect us both, and never feel any fear at all. We start to climb some way out of town, above the road where the Vajra Hotel is, and going even higher. This glorious feeling of flying through these beautiful surroundings, with incredible views across the valley, is something I will never forget. The sensation of freedom I get with my crimson cloak floating behind me. As we are still climbing, we drive through another small village and every other male is dressed in those glorious Buddhist monks' habits, deepest crimson over the saffron tunic. Finally we arrive at Monkey Temple. The bike is parked, and more steps face me...

We arrive at the first terrace with monkeys everywhere, and a young priest is silently praying with his small prayer book. By now the sun is warm, but the valley and Kathmandu itself are still shrouded in mist. The whole area of the mountainside and temple are covered in fluttering flags, showing fragments of the liturgy in Sanskrit. Climbing from one terrace to another there are more idols or statues. We pass a Peace pool with a goddess in the middle that has been given by Japan for world peace. The whole site covers the entire top of a very high hill, but the final level, where the main temple and 'stupa' are situated, is an amazing and totally unexpected delight. This is like another small village in the sky, with shops and people busy buying and selling, and practising rituals, all bathed in glorious sunshine far above the mist hanging in the valley. The temple building interior is glittering with tiny candles, and of course numerous very old wise-looking monks, inside and out, praying and meditating.

In the middle of the whole compound, overpowering everything else is an enormous stupa. My teacher, Prejwal, explains its meaning to me. The base, a big round white mound symbolises the earth. Over this is a square mound with the eyes of Buddha on every side. From this comes the tower, made up of thirteen stages to bring one to complete enlightenment, and consequently Nirvana.

While I'm up in that enchanting village in the sky, I use up every reel of film I have, and buy a typical Nepalese wall hanging, intricately embroidered in tiny seed pearls and sparkling sequins as a keepsake of that magical day."

Today it is a large cushion cover in my sitting room. Little do those who lean against it know it comes from somewhere over the rainbow, not in Hollywood, but from the holiest temple in Kathmandu.

On my last day, I ring Prejwal's home to leave a goodbye message. I have previously written a letter of gratitude for the wonderful week he has given me, and enclose a present that I know he would not accept from me in person. I half hope he might suddenly appear to say goodbye, but he doesn't. At the airport there are the usual delays and confusion about embarkation forms and immigration visas, and very little information. I ask a young man if this is the queue for Delhi, and he says, "Hallo Beth, do you remember me – David?" He's a young missionary I'd met in Harpenden at the YWAM campus. Now he's holding a baby. Then he says, "This is my wife, we're on our way to Thailand." His pretty wife looks either Nepali or most probably Thai (what a very small world we live in.)

On the plane, I am given an aisle seat. The man in the window seat asks me if I have ever been on this flight from Nepal before. I admit it is my first time, and he insists I must sit in his seat, to get a view of the Himalayas. I am virtually glued to the window. It's breathtaking, watching those magnificent peaks slowly glide by the plane, and the range seems to go on forever. Watching the sun gradually sink behind the grandeur and majesty of that unforgettable range, I remember the words from one of Madeleine l'Engle's beautiful books given to me when I first made 'The Choice'. '*When I think of the incredible, incomprehensible sweep of Creation above me, I have the strange reaction of feeling fully alive. Rather than feeling lost and unimportant and meaningless, set against galaxies, which go beyond the reach of the furthest telescopes, I feel that my life indeed has meaning. Perhaps I should feel insignificant, but instead I feel a soaring in my heart that the God who could create all this - and out of nothing- can still count the hairs on my head.*' Those words always brought tears to my eyes, and they still do.

How kind of my window-seat neighbour. I've been constantly blessed wherever I've gone on this new extraordinary journey. Now I am on my way home, back to London and Notting Hill to be re-united with family for Christmas 1998.

I wonder what the next step will be in this amazing 'Choice' I've been given....

22

THE KING'S LODGE

The next few months while waiting in London, I busy myself at St Peter's, and help to organise events with The Arts Centre Group, which uses one of the many offices in the Parish Hall as their Headquarters in the Portobello Road. They are a support-group for Christian artists (writers, actors, musicians and the visual arts). Artists of every discipline have a very solitary existence while writing, painting or just waiting for the next job or commission, and need every bit of support and encouragement they can get - as I know from painful experience. There is plenty to keep me busy and fulfilled. Yet there is that inner restlessness in me that I know so well. What is God trying to tell me?

In July I travel to Leith, teaching on a Drama Workshop at one of the YWAM bases just outside Edinburgh. An amazing young woman is the creator of the school. She also founded her own theatre company called The Cutting Edge Theatre Company. The YWAM School is quite small, but the students will be integrated with Suzanne's other local drama clubs, and have the chance to be part of the Edinburgh Festival. (She continues to write, direct and travel all over the world, bringing drama workshops to African villages, and last year in the USA, with prisoners in American jails!)

I'll always remember the sentence in her very first letter to me in 1999 "*I dream very big dreams Beth.*" I know then she's someone after my own heart. By the end of the summer, I again feel the need to work full-time in a community surrounded by other full-time Christians...but where? Suddenly two names from my first school in Hawaii ten years ago come to the surface of my memory - Jack and Dorothy - of course! They are now leading the large YWAM training campus in the Midlands. I remember it was on my first weekend visit there that those first nudges of excitement catapulted me into beginning this most unlikely 'Choice,' and changed my whole life as an actress, as I chose to try and become a dedicated Christian missionary at the age of sixty-three.

Without hesitating I lift the phone and call The King's Lodge. I know there are at least a couple of DTS training schools each year, as well as the School for Biblical Studies, a Preaching and Teaching School, and a Leadership Training School. It is very probable that they will be looking for staff members who have already gone through the training. My interview is with the young man who is leading the next DTS school, along with Kathryn the young woman who is in charge of the personnel department. Immediately I feel the same excitement I experienced there before, and hope they feel I'm a possible candidate.

I hear later that the answer I give to their question, "What reason do you have for wanting to come on staff," clinched their final decision: "Well next year I'm into my seventy-second birthday and I have a funny feeling that the Lord is going to keep me around until I am at least ninety-two. So I have another twenty years to be doing something for Him."

Whatever the reason is, I get that welcome letter to start in September. I mention that I'm already booked for a couple of talks for churches, as well as performing in an Arts Festival in Cambridge, organised by Arts in Mission, for the Millennium Year. They are happy to let me fulfil these commitments during the term, and wish me well. There is just one issue I admit I am not certain about. Apparently the normal commitment is for two years. I do not want to commit myself to more than this one experimental term, as I want to be sure that this is God leading me, and not just another of my own bright ideas. We eventually come to this agreement.

Saturday 18th of September 1999 is the first day of term, and reading my journal it brings back so many memories of those early days of being on school staff. My journal is in great detail as I'm so thrilled and excited about every single thing. Obviously I am not going to use each page to give you a day-to-day description of all my thoughts and activities during my next six years on staff, but these first few weeks of my journal are so revealing. I have since forgotten my reactions to this first term still being a very new Christian, and living alongside all these other members of the community who seem to have been believers forever. I have so much to learn. Let me quote one day of that first week....

Wednesday 22nd October. "This day our very dynamic school leader, Danie from South Africa, teaches about letting go and handing things over to God. He starts with David and his offering of those five small stones to slay Goliath. Next, Elisha and the widow with her tiny offering of oil that then multiplies to fill countless jars. Finally, he quotes the example of the young boy with his two fish and five loaves multiplying to feed five thousand. "What did Jesus have to hand over?" A box of nails is passed around. By this time the classroom is totally silent. A large cross is dragged in and propped against the wall. "So, what can you lay down, let go, what do you hold onto?" I immediately think of my lovely little flat in Notting Hill; all my friends in the church there, and all my life-long friends in theatre. I remember the directors who have given me such wonderful parts to play. The great reviews I nearly always had - a different life completely. And I take a great big breath. "Write them down, fold up the paper and leave it at the foot of the cross." During this time our young students are so silent, as each one slowly steps out with their slip of paper. Suddenly I hear a helpless sobbing coming from a young girl with her piece of paper in her hand, kneeling at the cross. I long to go out and comfort her, but realise that she's already being cared for by that Presence, which I know is in the classroom. Student after student is touched."

As someone steeped in the world of drama, I love the way these lessons are so often enacted.

The mornings start at 8.30 am, and very often the evenings continue well after 9 pm. High tea is around 5.00 pm, with the probability you are on wash-up in the kitchen. At 6.00 pm I'm ready to get back to my cosy bed-sit and put my feet up. It's an all-consuming day.

Another of my journal entries reads:

"At 7.30 pm, when I am longing to slip away to my room, I discover there's to be a bonfire evening. Tom (a rugged pioneering type American from Georgia) volunteers to set it up and rather reluctantly, I drag myself there. Then I see this wonderful picture: around forty people, silhouetted by an enormous bonfire with great logs six inches across. The students and staff are sitting in a circle on tree trunks and around picnic tables and their faces glow in the firelight. One of the staff has her guitar, and the sound of favourite worship songs fill this glorious starlit night. With a full moon above, it's magical - a gift.

After Danie throws all our little scraps of paper into the fire to be consumed, he explains that the evening was suggested during a prayer time before the term had even started, when someone quoted 'God is an all-consuming fire.' I really need to say a little prayer of thank you for showing me so many different ways to live my life for Him. Especially living in Community with my new family, sharing so much fun and joy. Back in my room I feel at home. There's light, warmth, my little bedside radio for music and news, and already even friendship in this first week, besides a purpose, which hasn't even started yet. It's not as beautiful as my home in Notting Hill, but that no longer satisfies me enough. I can only live each day and each week to the fullest. But for now it's time for bed and a good night's sleep. So thank you Father."

That first term up in the Midlands teaches me a great deal about myself. I also find myself falling in love with the lanes and fields of this unspectacular countryside on the Warwickshire/Leicestershire border. Watling Street (or the A5) was originally built by the Romans, as I know so well from my school days back in St Albans, (original site of the Roman city of Verulamium). It's also the border between the two counties. Nuneaton, Coventry and all roads leading to Stratford on Avon and Warwick itself are to the west, but turn to the east and you see the much smaller towns and villages: Higham on the Hill and Stoke Golding (near where the Battle of Bosworth was fought) eventually leading to the medieval market town of Leicester. These market towns and villages were part of the industrial revolution, and around the late 19th century were involved in leather manufacturing (footwear mainly), and the hosiery industry.

I also begin to discover that I'm becoming a lover of the countryside and its way of life.

My final quote from my journal written while living at The King's Lodge in the first few weeks:

"SUNDAY MORNING: I'm writing this in bed, facing my vast picture window, which looks out to an even vaster sky. Here in this simple room I wake up each morning to God's sky, with all its variations. Usually I

hear next door's farm cows mooing away, but this morning I only hear the rooks cawing in the treetops. I've been pondering about the simplicity of my life here. How different it is from Notting Hill with the constant socialising, and doing things up in my flat. That used to be my comfort zone, and moving up here was to be my courage zone. Strangely though, this now feels more like my comfort zone. Working here has its challenges of course, but virtually living in one room, and having all my meals provided simplifies life, so that there is more time to study and learn, to read and write and think and pray. It's quite monastic, and what could be better in my seventies to live like this, clearing my life for Jesus, I find myself wanting to know MORE, hopefully getting closer to Him so that more gets rubbed off onto me. I'm learning to grow in patience and understanding and non-judgmentally, learning to clear out more garbage, and leaving the channels open to His love for me and for others. It's this that will give me happiness, rather than finding fault with the pattern of the carpet, and the excruciatingly bright blue painted radiator and windowsill! Just seeing that sky, and watching the birds as they wheel across the roof to the trees. Watching the clouds moving in slow motion from one side of the window to the other.

I discover more of Nuneaton on its colourful, bustling market day. Most of the town centre is pedestrianised, and, to remind us that this is the birthplace of George Eliot (1819-1888), there is a statue of her right in the middle of the market square. We studied "Silas Marner" at school, but I have to admit I haven't read any more of her many novels since. I had better find the public library. There's an enormous amount for me to discover about this Middle England."

Looking back at those words, I wonder at the idealism and pure naivety, especially the *growing in patience and understanding and non-judgmentally.* How long, dear Lord, how long? I am reminded of my irate reaction to my teenage granddaughters visiting me here at Christmas. Their television choices from 'Top of The Pops' onwards through the evening so irritate me that eventually I rebel and pretend I am longing to watch a film in Hindi with English sub-titles. I'm met with squeals of indignation and slammed doors, and pained faces from their parents. How about that first lesson on Handing Things Over, and the other wonderful week's teaching on Relinquishing Your Rights! I remember saying at my first interview, "I think He is going to keep me busy down here until I am at least ninety-two!" He knows how long it's all going to take. But I digress....

I live in community at The King's Lodge for the next three and a half years, and during this time I not only help to staff the schools, I start looking for a different challenge. Loving books, I volunteer to take over the management of the bookshop on the campus. I also realise that many people in Nuneaton and its surroundings are unsure as to what "*that big red school building on Watling Street is all about*". Perhaps I can be a sort of Ambassador, talking to various groups about the different schools and activities that take place here? I'm given the positive go-ahead.

To work in the bookshop I have to become computer literate. Thankfully Eileen Jackson, the previous manager, teaches me the basics. How does she ever have the patience to put up with my total ignorance of this mysterious machine? Her loving care and perseverance is only one of the many qualities, which endear her to me. Realising however, that I also need the back up of some formal classes in IT, I sign on at the local Nuneaton College for a beginners' class, one morning a week, which I love, but also find frustrating. In this large class I am constantly waiting with my hand up, begging for help. Gradually though the mist begins to clear, and I am nearly in control of this inanimate object, that is taking up so much of my life.

Apart from the bookshop, I begin to get invitations to speak to different church groups about our work at The King's Lodge, and I start building bridges by inviting them back to come and have a tour around the building. They are offered afternoon teas, and the chance to talk to different members of staff about their specific ministry. We also use the opportunity for them to hear from staff and students about their experiences on the mission field. The local vicar at Higham on the Hill, our nearest village, arranges for me to spend one morning a week at the Primary School, helping the small five year olds with their reading. They are very mystified about the way I speak without the local accent. I remember one little girl saying: "You speak funny don't you."

I reply, "I suppose I do. You see I come from a long way away - down in London." I become so fond of these children, and I learn so much from the school staff: just five of us, having tea breaks in the small staff room. Most of them live in the Leicestershire villages nearby, with much tougher lives than either I, or any of my friends in Notting Hill are used to. I am beginning to understand how narrow my life has been. There is also quite a lot of confusion in the village as to whether The King's Lodge is some sort of cult or sect, so I volunteer to write a page each month in the village magazine. I call this 'The King's Lodge Ledger' and it becomes a regular monthly article, read by most of the village community. They enjoy reading about some of our day-to-day activities, as well as the exciting adventures that students experience on outreach while away in some far-flung corners of the world.

By the time I'm seventy-six, I long to be back on school staff again, maybe for the last time, before I decide to call it a day. I am with a Crossroads Discipleship Training School (CDTS) - a mixed-age group, including parents with their children of all ages from toddlers to teens. It's agreed that I need only be on the staff of the school during the twelve weeks of classroom study. I am not expected to deal with the rigours of long haul flights, and the unknown conditions of the accommodation in some remote outpost on the mission field. I feel very happy with this, and as yet we have no idea where the Lord will be calling us on outreach. As it transpires this is one of the most memorable schools I staff, and when it is decided that we are going to the YWAM base on the island of Mindanao, in the Philippines, my mind is definitely made up. Yes! Apparently it seems God wants me to go with them. It's such a happy staff team, led by an Australian guy, who has the same gift of affirming students and staff that I found in my very first school with the inspirational Danie from South Africa. Our staff meetings with Chris are full of laughs. He always gives us the assurance that all is going well, that he has total confidence in the team around him - including me. This feeling permeates the whole school, and it's one of the happiest experiences of being on school staff I can remember.

Chris's wife, Cindee, will be travelling with us, with their two adorable little boys. A number of those students have since chosen to return as permanent staff members at the King's Lodge or at other YWAM communities elsewhere after the outreach. This is probably proof of the success of that school in 2004. For me it is one of the most glorious experiences of all my years with YWAM. I admit our accommodation has a lot to be desired. I am on the lower bunk in a dormitory shared with the five Filipino women staff. There is air-conditioning, and an adjoining shower room and lavatory. This is something I had earnestly prayed for, as my water-works are showing their age...but I didn't think of praying for a lavatory that works! Oh well, to begin with it has to be flushed by pouring buckets down, until one of our clever American guys employed in maintenance, finds the spare part that is needed, and all is well.

There are so many different ministries waiting for us. I choose to work with the local school children: about eighty of them. They come to the base on a Saturday morning, and hear stories, sing songs and make little crafts to take home as gifts. It is like any Sunday school in the UK except we teach alongside their Filipino teachers, acting as interpreters. The children are enchanting, eager to take part in everything, with wide cheeky grins and enormous brown eyes filled with mischief.

My seventy-sixth birthday takes place while I am out here, and this is celebrated during a school class, with much singing of 'Happy Birthday Mamma Beth', and hugs all round. After this, whenever I am seen in the surrounding squatters villages, I'm followed by shouts of "Mamma Beth - Happy Birthday." I feel totally overflowing with the love given to me from these children and their parents. Sadly we never seem to show this to each other over here in the Western world.

Although I am tempted to staff just one more school after this, the trip to the Philippines proves to be my last mission adventure with The King's Lodge. I discover that as much as I love the heat and humidity of these islands, my body is beginning to rebel. On my return, the visit to my trusted village doctor confirms that I have a condition that is exacerbated in those temperatures. This is a sad day, but I can find plenty to do here.

There is another surprise when I'm asked

to give up my beloved room at The King's Lodge. It is needed for two of our young members of staff who are now married. To begin with, I'm heartbroken to lose my precious room (my comfort zone) that has become home to me. Is this a sign pointing me back to my flat in Notting Hill? While I'm trying to make a decision, I get an unexpected phone call. A wonderful old lady in her late eighties makes the decision for me. Dorothy is a member of the Higham village church, who walks there in sunshine or rain, in spite of her age and her severely diminished eyesight. Over the phone, I hear her tremulous voice telling me of a village friend who needs to sell urgently, as her husband has suddenly been moved to a new job on the East Coast. The house has not even been put on the market yet, and knowing my love for the village, she feels I might like to have a look at it. This is such an extraordinary coincidence. No one up in Higham knows of my predicament. It is a definite nudge to make further enquiries, which I do. Consequently I make up my mind to move off the campus and into the village of Higham on the Hill, just up the road.

23

VILLAGE LIFE

It's the garden that really sells me the house. Originally designed by a landscape gardener, it leads away from the wide sliding picture windows from a sunny terrace up three ascending circular levels to a final shady oasis under large trees at the very end of the garden. I buy a couple of stone benches and set a stone cherub birdbath under the trees. Here is a place of peace and shade at the end of a summer's day. A place to sit and relax, to dream a little, while the birds start singing their goodnight songs before going to bed.

This is my first move into the world of country villages and their communities, and I am only a mile away from all my colleagues and friends down the hill at King's Lodge.

There is a small wooden gate at the end of the garden, which leads into the village recreation ground, and at the cost of half a crown in old money (50p nowadays), I am granted the right of way to take the short cut into the village centre. This payment is to be made every three years! My next door neighbour is the churchwarden of the village church. So many times as I draw my curtains back in the morning I see Margaret trudging across the Rec, with or without her umbrella, always faithful and uncomplaining, and only a few years my junior.

Now I am away from the close-knit community of The King's Lodge and the structured daily living, I find living alone without a regular nine to five commitment needs a new self-imposed motivation. I still keep to my morning quiet time and often find my inspiration for the day ahead from those daily Bible studies. My creative juices occupy me by turning my small, undistinguished 1970s semi into a backdrop for my own personality. With the help of local painters, decorators, builders, plumbers, plasterers and electricians, I am opening my little home up to light and sunshine. Bright new paintwork with colours of my choice, echoing those I had lived with in London, make me feel at home again. These first couple of years keep me busy and happy. Being so close to the campus, I am also able to continue part-time with the school. I have the added joy of the students' small group meetings at my home. I can still keep that close friendship with them, following their progress through the term as I've always done before.

I always believe that there must be *something more* just around the corner. This is a restlessness that never allows me to be totally content to stay in one place. Maybe the years I spent working in the world of theatre have contributed to this desire to move on. Touring the country with a play for maybe twelve weeks is not a favourite contract for many actors. For me it's an endless delight. I love staying in one town for just one week, always looking forward to what is waiting for us next. When we are in towns with beautiful cathedrals to be explored and antique shops to rummage through, I am in my element. I have a whole week to explore, with so many new discoveries to pack away in my memories. By Friday evening, after the curtain, I am already starting to collect my dressing room bits and pieces together. I'm ready for the *get out* after Saturday's two shows, saying goodbyes and thank-you to my theatre digs landlady, and all the friendly and helpful theatre staff. I'm impatient for the drive home to London and the children. They will be waiting for the presents I always buy with my pay packet as a guilt offering for being away.

In the past, I was always on the move, just long enough to be with people to make a charming but superficial impression, but never long enough to go any deeper into others' lives. I expect this is one of the reasons that attracts me to short-term mission trips. It is easier than making that dangerous commitment of staying in one place, one church, one community and having to put roots deep down. So, even now, I know in my heart that my small village home is not my final move. I am still yearning for that *something more*, the ultimate something that I can't explain, even to myself.

I remember having those longings for that indefinable something many years ago. It was at Salisbury Playhouse. I was rehearsing "Cider with Rosie", a play filled with lyrical poetry; learning the central and heart-warming part of Laurie Lee's mother. I loved to drive out to those beautiful Wiltshire chalk downs after rehearsals. One afternoon I stood completely alone, high on the downs looking across a valley with fields of golden corn and scarlet poppies, endless blue skies above, and hearing the song of a skylark high, so high above me. I want to hold on to that beauty forever, and the tears start to fall as the deepest part of me is yearning for that *something more* People say that there is a big round hole inside one, where God is meant to be. I think back to '*The Choice*' and ponder the years of my life since the horror and pain of Adam's violent death. So much of the life I was leading before that dreadful day has been stripped away. I no longer yearn to be given a new script, to be offered a wonderful new part, for that something which might just eventually lead to celebrity and fame and the top of the tree! Now it's for something else.

I still haven't let my London home go. Janet, my lovely tenant, has always been reliable in every way. Her rent has been an enormous help while I'm working with YWAM, especially now that I am back living in the real world. While in The King's Lodge, everything is provided: all lighting, heating, food, and community tax, as part of my staff fees. Now all these bills are my responsibility. I definitely still need Janet. I like my little semi, and now that I have totally refurbished it, there is nothing else I need.

The family is only able to visit a couple of times a year, but that's normal as they live far away in Sussex. I no longer enjoy driving that distance, but always take the train for any of my son Hugo's events in Horsham, where he has created a Performing Arts

Centre, attached to their church building, which he calls 'The Space'. Often he asks me to be involved in various shows he has written. Once he devises a poignant nostalgic family show using all of us. He somehow persuades his father to be part of it as well, having written a very funny sketch about Adam and Eve, on Adam's one hundred and fifth birthday, when Eve has given him an apple for his birthday present. This opens the evening, using Jimmy as Adam and myself as Eve. It's a cleverly written comedy sketch, and a delight to play. I often use Eve's monologue when I'm asked to contribute to some entertainment. It's useful for an actress in her eighties! The rest of the show is made up of musical items from Rachel, my violinist daughter-in-law, and with my two musical granddaughters on violin and cello. Poetry and Irish stories come from Jimmy. Hugo is blessed with a lovely singing voice, and so is Rachel. There are solos and duets from all of them. I adore doing a hilarious Joyce Grenfell sketch, which always has everyone in stitches. I've never been able to resist getting the laughs. We finish with the final scene from "The Cherry Orchard" with all of us in it.

With one thing and another, I'm kept busy and happy. So why am I still restless? Where is that *something more?* I already seem to have everything: friends, family, a warm happy church, and especially a very loving daughter who is trying to cope with an unhappy marriage for the sake of her small son. They are both living in the next village. I long to have that total peace which is so perfectly described in Psalm131: *...like a weaned child with its mother, like a weaned child is my soul within me.* It would help if I even knew what I am looking for. I know that travelling to the other side of the world with YWAM teams is no longer realistic. I am going to have to think laterally about my future activities. I begin exploring all the country lanes and villages here in Leicestershire, and discover the many barn conversions. The financial problems that so many farmers are facing mean they are also being forced to think laterally and diversify. Many of their old barns are no longer being used for their original purposes. There also seems to be a longing among many city folk to get out of the rat race: to sell up and move out to small villages and try rural life. Developers soon get wind of this current trend, and each redundant barn is being transformed into every townie's dream home.

The feeling I first had when I moved into my small semi in Higham village remains with me. This is only going to be my first stepping–stone into the real world again. It is only to be a path to another crossroads, leading to another 'choice'. A choice between staying, or going back to my former comfort zone of Notting Hill, and joining all my old friends at St Peter's again, where God first stepped firmly into my life.

I begin looking at these barn conversions more seriously; this time for myself, for this townie. If I can find that perfect place, a place that outshines 'Clearings', my small garden flat in London, then I will know God wants me to stay here, and let London go. Yes... still another layer of letting go. A very large early Victorian building on the top of a hill, just as you are entering the next village, keeps attracting me. Stoke Golding is a village which proclaims itself to be "*The Birthplace* of *the Tudor* Dynasty". This handsome building I discover has actually been the hub of the village's hosiery industry in the late nineteenth century. According to a short history I am given, titled "*250 Million Pairs of Sock,*" production began in 1882, basically to produce thick woollen socks to keep the feet of farmers warm and dry as they worked all the hours God sends. These socks soon begin to be in demand in farming communities all around Europe. They also supply the British troops in two world wars. By the seventies and eighties, however, factories in Asia and China begin producing similar products, but much cheaper. The village factory is gradually closed, the staff are made redundant, and this fine old building lies empty. In the nineties, long before the current trend of barn conversions, a clever London developer sees the potential, and the present building now called 'The Courtyard' is re-born.

Offering twelve newly designed Luxury Apartments, the building first catches my eye soon after my move from London, while living in The King's Lodge. Whenever a For Sale sign appears, I immediately get in touch with the Estate Agent, mainly out of curiosity. I fall in love with every flat I look at, and the prices, in comparison with Notting Hill, are ludicrous: well within my budget. However, although I see four different flats, they are either on the upper floor with rather too many stairs to climb, or they are on the side of the building that only has a view into the main courtyard. I always have that little internal nudge, which says *wait!* I yearn for that view from the top of the hill right over the fields. So I obey that whispered *wait.*

By the time I start getting itchy feet at my little semi in Higham, I start exploring the lanes and nearby villages, discovering all the newly converted barns. One glorious summer afternoon I see a new development of four barn conversions in the next village of Dadlington. They have enormous potential I think, overlooking fields that seem to go on forever without a building in sight. Nothing but green and the bright yellow of rape fields in the spring, right down to the canal. I drive over, park the car and walk into the paved yard. To my great disappointment, they all face inwards to the yard, and there are large farm buildings at the back to block that wondrous view. Sadly I drive away back to my little semi, going past 'The Courtyard'. There is a new For Sale sign outside, but I ignore it and drive on until the bottom of the hill. Then I distinctly feel that nudge again. Turning the car round, I drive back up the hill and note the flat number – No 7. In the car park a young woman is cleaning her car and I ask her, which is No 7. She drops her pail and sponge, taking me round to the side of the house, which looks right over the valley to the horizon and the hills of Higham. French windows are wide open, and the owner of No 7 is sitting on his patio enjoying the sun. I apologise for just walking in unannounced but he laughs, saying that the board has only just gone up that day!

"Would you like to have a quick look

round?"

"Yes please" and in we go. Bells start to ring in my head. This is my new home. All the other flats have been *possibles*, but that small voice said: *wait*. Now I hear *yes this is it*. Turning to my host, I say how much I love it, and I'll be in touch with the agent immediately for the details, and for a formal viewing. In a couple of days my offer is accepted. I put the Higham on the Hill house on the market, ring my wonderful financial wizard to let him know what I am doing...and ask is it feasible? This is where another enormous *letting go* is to be made. The London flat needs to be sold. Am I sure that I'm ready to cut that last lifeline, the final umbilical cord, to my beloved London? I am horrified at the thought: "But surely the rent that I get from London makes it still worth keeping on." – and - "It is so nice to know that it is still there, and I can always pop back and forth."

By this time my son and daughter are involved. "But Mum, you can't live in it while you are renting it out. You can only live there if you stop renting, if you sell up where you are and decide to go back - finally. "

My heart says "No! No, No, I can't leave London." Then I remember the line "you'll never believe the freedom you'll find from the things you leave behind." Michael Card, a popular Christian songwriter's lyric, was to help me once before when throwing all my old diaries out. I kept trying to bring them in from the bins, before the bin-men collected them. I was in a complete panic about letting them go, but I felt such a sense of freedom when they'd gone.

But leaving a city where roots have gone down so deep, where my friends, and a way of life, and memories of over twenty years have been made; that is a big ask until I am totally certain that No 7 The Courtyard, Stoke Golding is where my next move is meant to be. I toss the question backwards and forwards. Is this God's plan? Unlike Higham, where wallpapers of dubious designs were rapidly stripped off, and the whole house re-painted and completely redesigned, No 7 is closer to everything I have ever longed for.

Those high, high ceilings. As high as Holland Park's. The pale wooden floors. The Shaker (or is it Quaker?) kitchen, with its Belfast sink. The wonderful feeling of space and light. The open-plan design, with only one step up from drawing room to dining area.

And those views! At long last I am in real country, no longer in that tidy little suburban semi. I want to just move in, and bring everything I've ever owned from London, W11. From Holland Park Avenue, Lonsdale Road and lastly Chepstow Place W2. I long to be surrounded by my much loved sofas, my beautiful chaise-longue, the satinwood kneehole desk, all bought while still married to Jimmy, as well as all the other beautiful antiques I've always collected over the span of my life.

I hope my past acquisitive lifestyle is being forgiven. Like our Creator, I confess I also do love beautiful things.

First Christmas @ my Sock Factory.

My 80th birthday - lots of fun and silliness, in our cabaret.

Hugo missing.

24

MY SOCK FACTORY AND 80TH BIRTHDAY

No 7 The Courtyard becomes mine on 6th October 2006: nine years ago. There are many changes to my life. Living in a small Leicestershire village isn't as adventurous as those years of travelling all over the world, and it doesn't have the glamour, flattery, fun and friendship from all those years on stage. Life in my eighties is very different: *To everything there is a Season. A time for every purpose under Heaven.* Ecclesiastes 3. Although I have very little idea what my *purpose* is meant to be. Instead of keeping my old descriptive journals, I'm now a member of our local village magazine's editorial team. Each month I have the joy of finding one of the older residents, and asking them for their life story for 'Beth's Corner' in our magazine.

One of the things that delights me is how positive my entire family is about my new home. I remember my son Hugo's comment on the wooden shutters to my bedroom windows and how he is going to paint them a contrasting colour to my walls. (They're still unpainted). Someone else remarks as they walk through from the car-park, "*it's like entering another world.*" Even my dear ex thoroughly approves. I've always known that they were all a bit disappointed with my little semi: "*it's not really you Beth.*" Well no, Higham didn't compete with London, but this is totally different. I have never lived in a property that doesn't look out onto a street. Green fields, which stretch to the horizon, surround me on two sides. I am also enchanted by the flock of Jacob sheep we have in our adjoining meadows. When they were really small in springtime, a particularly adventurous lamb scrambled under the wooden fence to eat the flowers and the greener grass on our lawn. He is a special pet, with a sweet little black face. The fields beyond are home to much larger flocks of less memorable sheep, without the piebald effect of our Jacob's.

Although I no longer have those extensive, detailed pages of memories, there are one or two intermittent passages that I've just come across. These are in a couple of beautiful books that friends have given me as 'moving in' presents, knowing how much I always enjoy scribbling. Sadly, I find that the more I come to terms with the laptop, the less time I spend scribbling in my notebooks. There are one or two accounts that really give an idea of how positive I feel about having made the final choice of letting go of 'Clearings' my little garden flat in London. They are worth quoting:

"When I open the shutters of my bedroom at 7.30 this morning, I am faced with one of the reasons why I am so content to be living here on the top of my hill. The scene is breath-takingly beautiful. The vast canopy of sky we have is early morning's

deepest blue with no other building anywhere to block it. Across the fields and the valley, thin wreaths of gauze mists are lying, waiting to be lifted by the strengthening Spring sun. Oh yes! This is HOME."

Another entry is in January and I've written:

"...is a morning of frozen landscape, white and fogbound, where nothing is visible beyond our fence. We might as easily be located on the edge of a cliff!! For two or three days I've had the feeling that the Earth is in the grip of The White Queen as in Narnia: everything seems silent and dead."

Always having lived in central London, I've no idea I will respond with such delight to this rural living. The village has its own small Post Office and we are all encouraged to sign up on the petition that comes through our letterboxes, demanding it shall not be closed. We are lucky, but Higham just a mile away has lost theirs. We have our own village surgery, and I volunteer to be one of the emergency drivers, and take prescriptions to disabled patients who are housebound. I'll always remember delivering a stack of tablets to one of the nearby villages, and as the patient comes to the door to sign the necessary form, my journal notes: *"I'm appalled at the lady's swollen limbs. Poor love – what a life. How can she believe in a God of Love?"*

I notice that many of the other entries deal with my visits as part of the Hospital Chaplaincy team. Before living in this village, I trained with the very large Nuneaton hospital, named after George Eliot. I worked there for a number of years, just once a week, as part of a large Multi-Faith team. Now I am visiting in our local Sunnyside Hospital, about six minutes' drive away. This is primarily for the rehabilitation of the elderly after they've been treated at the big General Hospitals for strokes, falls, or heart conditions. Sunnyside is a delight after the unending corridors of the large city hospitals. Most of the patients are in single rooms with their own en-suite facilities, and it is a modern building; light and airy. I become so fond of some of the elderly, I long to follow their progress when they return home, so often to living alone. When I broach this subject with the hierarchy, I am assured this is not part of the job, as it might offend family members. This closeness of family is something else I learn about these rural villages. Quite often whole families still live in the village they were born in, with two or three generations nearby, never moving away. Once in one of the acute family suites, I notice at least three generations gathered around the bed of an elderly patient in a coma. As I pass the room again on my way out, a young woman is standing outside the door sobbing. I stop and gently putting my arm on her shoulder, ask her if it is her Mum who is so very poorly. "*No it's my Nan.*" Her small children are in the room with the rest of the family. We say a little prayer for Nan and for Peace for them all. I am so moved by their love for each other.

The family suites are a godsend for patients and their families. Apart from the normal en-suite facilities, there is a separate kitchen, a cosy sofa bed in a curtained alcove, and French windows opening onto a small private terrace. I tease the nursing staff, saying I'm only doing this job because I'm keeping one eye on my own future needs

I am determined to make my big 80 an event I will never forget. After moving here, we become great friends with a family from church who constantly invite numerous people in for meals! Martyn adores cooking, and he and his wife Jo have a gift for hospitality. He offers to organise a hog roast for me, saying he and a friend have often done it before. The idea of seeing the body of a pig being slowly cooked over a roasting spit doesn't fit the image in my mind, especially as there are bound to be children running around. Instead I remember once many years ago in Cyprus at Easter time. The day before fasting for Lent, whole families meet for an enormous communal picnic. The smell of lamb and rosemary and other spices hang in the air. This always reminds me of the Mediterranean and the joy of sunny outdoors living. I start looking up Greek restaurants, and only find one in Tamworth, about fourteen miles away.

It is one of the best decisions I have ever made. Christos and his brother are jewels. They bring all their stuff over, set up the barbecues for the portions of lamb, which have been marinating since the day before. Salads, dolmades, pitta, humus and tzatziki are all laid out, while we have the time to welcome and chat to our guests. Over ninety friends are able to accept.

The greatest miracle is the weather. It has been appalling for weeks: great cloudbursts of rain and gales, with the forecast of continuing low pressure. There is nothing I can do about it! The weather is God's domain - so I leave it to Him! The morning dawns with bright sunshine and stays that way all day. A number of folk even opt for sitting under the gazebo to protect them from the heat. My sister-in-law becomes quite cross with me when I say God wants me to have a wonderful day, and has planned the good weather in answer to my prayers. She mutters about the absurdity of it – 'what about everyone else's prayers?'

Everyone is ecstatic over the wonderful kleftiko and mezes, asking Christos how he has cooked the lamb and made the dolmades, and now the children want to go indoors where all the desserts are lined up along the length of the dining table. But as usual Hugo arranges a family Cabaret to be performed from the patio steps. I fight against this, saying everyone will be bored stiff, but he insists. So I announce we are having a cabaret first, "It is Showtime"! Infuriatingly, Hugo is proved to be right, as usual.

We have a wonderful audience all sitting in their garden chairs, and on picnic rugs, right in front of us, apparently rapt by our amazing talent! They love the idea that my ex, whom they all know from television, is taking part, apparently with good grace. Hugo has always been good at twisting the occasional arm, including those belonging to every member of the family. I think one of the highlights is my then ten-year old granddaughter playing a violin duet with her professional violinist mother. Naturally we focus on comedy, but there is music; Shakespeare's 'Seven Ages of Man' and a lot of silliness and laughter. Then, and only then, comes the rush for puddings. So many friends who have come to help me celebrate this special birthday surround me, and again I feel that 'the choice' to leave Notting Hill and to become an in-comer to this small Midland village has been the right one.

In the early summer evening, when most of the guests are gone, I watch the sun as it sets over the horizon, as usual, with its glorious streaks of pinks and purples across the darkening night.

Relaxing around the lawn and under the trees, with the family and a few remaining friends who all helped to make my day so special, we taste the heady delights of our success - along with the cold white wine still left in the fridge.

25

HUGO & 'THE SPACE'

Hugo's talent as a performer, and even more perhaps as an instigator, touches many people's lives. He is so totally determined when he has his mind made up about presenting his many shows at 'The Space' in Horsham or elsewhere. One Easter show in particular, I remember how he harasses an actress about taking part. She insists she doesn't feel confident enough, and she hasn't done anything for ages - so "thank you Hugo, but no thank you." Eventually she gives in and has to play opposite me in a very aggressive scene as my daughter–in-law, and is brilliant. Afterwards in a highly emotional state, she comes to me and I hug her: "Aren't you glad Hugo persuaded you?" He has this extraordinary gift for knowing how wonderful people can be if they are challenged.

Another talent is for putting a programme together. I have an example of one in front of me right now entitled "Visions in the Wilderness," another of his Space Projects for the season of Lent. This involves six weekends of Art & Spirituality, ranging from film, poetry, visual art, a classical concert; and an evening of theatrical excerpts that I've just referred to, which he calls 'Under a Spotlight'. The smaller blurb explaining the contents of the evening states: *'Scenes from recent hits of the London, and New York stage.'* *"Religion'"* *by Mick Gordon and A C Grayling explores the conflict between science and faith. "The last days of Judas Iscariot" by Stephen Adley Guirgis is a hilarious and extraordinary courtroom drama where history's most infamous betrayal is dissected by the forces of good and evil.* <u>*Some scenes contain strong language.'*</u> The underlining is mine. He sends me the various scripts, presumably for my affirmation. I phone him immediately to say I am appalled that he's considering allowing such disgusting language to be uttered in front of a Christian audience. As usual he pacifies me by saying he has cleared it with his long-suffering vicar, and anyway it is being performed in the wonderful new Community Hall, not in the actual church itself. His long-suffering vicar was persuaded the year before to play one of the lovers in "A Midsummer Night's Dream" opposite Hugo's wife. (Their love scene causes a delighted response from his congregation).

When it comes to the evening of this performance in question, I sit mesmerized. He persuades two of the professional actors who teach in his Drama department at Hurtwood House to play Judas and Jesus. It is electrifying. The audience is riveted. Jesus is desperately trying to convince Judas in purgatory that He still loves him and everything is forgiven, but Judas is unable to receive this and keeps telling Him to "F... off" again and again. I have never seen a scene between two actors played with such honesty and power. Again I'm forced to admit "Wow he was right." I am so very proud of my son and his radical vision for the Arts in Christianity.

The character I have to perform is from the same play. I am the mother of Judas Iscariot. The opening lines of the speech are: "*No parent should have to bury a child. Mothers are not meant to bury sons. It is not in the natural order of things. I buried my son. In a potter's field. In a field of blood. In empty acrid silence. There was no funeral. There were no mourners. His friends all absent. His father dead. His sisters refused to attend.*" I remember his close friend Simon saying how cruel of Hugo, but I know Hugo has given it to me, because I have already buried my son. I can take this woman's pain as if it is my own, albeit in very different circumstances. The instinct of an actor is to use everything life throws at them as grist for the mill.

My next skirmish with him a couple of years later involves an even greater battle of wills. It involves us performing a two-hander before an audience made up of the enthusiasts that attend the annual summer school run by the very excellent performing arts organization Riding Lights. I sign on along with Hugo, for the Creative Writing classes. Charlotte, Hugo's elder daughter is also going for one of the teenage acting workshops. I am thrilled that three generations of the Ellis family are going to enjoy a creative arts holiday together in beautiful Yorkshire. Then like a bolt from the blue I receive a script, with a perfunctory note explaining that this has been written by one of the members of The Space Theatre Group. Hugo has been encouraging his friend Simon to persevere with his writing skills. It needs an elderly actress to play the part of an ageing Christina Rossetti, close to her deathbed. I know they have become fascinated with the lives of her brother Dante Gabriel Rossetti and the others of the Pre-Raphaelite Brotherhood, but this is the first hint that I am now expected to take on the role of Christina Rossetti.

I tentatively look at the first page. This consists of a monologue, setting the scene, all spoken by Christina. I swiftly leaf through the next forty or so pages, and I decide quite definitely, this is beyond me. Ringing Hugo, I am pleasant but adamant. There's no way I can learn this length of a part any longer. In the past I was known for learning lines in lengthy roles, sometimes taking over for others who chickened out. After all I was raised in the school of theatre, now long gone, known as weekly rep. I continue arguing that I am now in my eighties, and what is more, totally out of practice. It is out of the question!! I repeat the lecture that we (the Chaplaincy team) have recently attended, on senile dementia. How that little piece in the brain, which makes memory, starts to fail in the ageing process.

He suggests rather sharply that I might start taking cod liver oil tablets. Then comes the next bombshell. He's already told Paul Burbridge (the founder of Riding Lights) that we will be performing this, and he is already slotting us in for one of the evening's performances. There seems to be no escape unless I fall out with both Hugo and Simon, and let them down in front of Paul. The fact that we live a hundred and fifty miles apart from each other is another small problem that I tentatively mention. Does he anticipate any rehearsals at all together? "Oh don't worry Ma! As soon as I break up from school I'll nip up for a few days. In the meantime you just get on with the lines." Oh well...I reconcile myself to the bad old days of learning lines! I set four hours apart each day and stick at the script.

Apart from a weekend of pruning some of the speeches, we only have four full days during the holidays, rehearsing together at our local church hall in the village. During that time, Hugo also insists on getting small props to dress the set. So we are visiting antique shops in surrounding villages for these. Finally we need to hire a Victorian vicar's outfit for my (six foot four inch) son with the help of the wardrobe mistress from a nearby drama company. I rustle up my own Victorian garments from my existing wardrobe, and that is it! I have never been so terrified about a performance (in spite of copious prayers from both Hugo and Amanda, assuring me God is always faithful!!) From that day on I go over my words every morning as I wake up, and again in the evening before I go to bed, including the night before the performance itself.

The stage management and lighting team are an enormous help to us, and the imaginative open setting for Rossetti's study looks stunning. The darkened auditorium is packed with all the enthusiastic actors, writers and drama teachers taking part in this week's workshops. They will all be presenting the plays they have been working on during the following two nights. We are the premiere.

I sit in the dark at Rossetti's desk before the stage is lit, praying, and as the lights reveal me, I suddenly feel as calm and sure of myself as if I have never stopped my acting career. From that moment, something switches on inside me, and I am away - flying again, such bliss! Christina has eventually *been born'* and is passionately telling her story to this dry Anglican priest who is harassing her to make her last confessions before her oncoming death. She's withstanding all his demands with such clarity, refusing to be drawn into his legalism and religiosity. I am revelling in the quick-fire thrust between Hugo and myself. We are well matched. Simon's dialogue has also come brilliantly alive. Reaching the climax when Christina breaks down in the middle of a long and painful memory of the past, the tears flow spontaneously. I share Christina's pain. We have done it, Hugo and me. It's as if we are back at The Everyman Theatre in Cheltenham, playing mother and son in Ibsen's "Ghosts" with Oswald dying in my arms. That is over twenty years ago, but Hugo has been proved right yet again.

After the curtain, I hug him in gratitude for his faith in me. It is an experience I will never forget, and I realise if it hadn't been for that arm-twisting, encouraging and visionary son of mine, I would have missed out.

The whole family comes up to be with me for Christmas 2010. On Christmas Eve we go to Leicester for the big musical "The King and I". It is very lusciously staged, with all the old well-remembered songs. I always book seats that include one on the aisle to allow Hugo to stretch his long legs. When I protest that I intentionally mean the aisle seat is for him, I'm touched and also a little puzzled when he insists on sitting next to me instead. On Christmas Day all seven of us fill an entire pew in church together. What more can any mother and grandmother want? My cup runneth over, although we still have the usual arguments about the number of television programmes they are intent on watching.

When I grumpily go to my room with a book, Hugo again leaves the others, and sits on the end of my bed to talk, and so quietly... "Why Mum do you make such an issue over these things. Why can't you just let them do what pleases them?" I have no recollection of my answer. I just remember being so happy that he is in the room with me, having a wonderful mother and son conversation together, instead of watching the television with them. Who is this newly gentle loving son who is giving me so much of himself?

I'm so sad to see them all go the following day - on to visit Rachel's side of the family, her Mum and Dad, sisters and brothers and scores of cousins. Perhaps at Easter we'll meet up again? In the meantime, they are going to be busy at Horsham rehearsing the first full-length play Hugo's written, about Vaughan Williams called "A Pilgrim's Song". He is always in the middle of something to do with The Space Theatre Company, as well as constantly writing and re-writing his memoirs "A Creative Journey" (Sub-titled "Rehearsing the Divine Drama of Life"). I remember an e-mail from Rachel, commenting that it's amazing after sitting so long working on his laptop he doesn't get a *numb bum!* He is obviously intent on finishing this memoir as soon as he can.

A few weeks after Christmas he sends me the first part, asking me to read it, and to let him know if I think there is any way he has misrepresented either myself or his father, and it is during our conversation that he suddenly says: *"Mum I think I'm going into another blip."*

26

'HUGO MISSING'

The first e-mail I receive reads as follows:

"Hi there. Sorry to say that Hugo has gone missing from lunchtime. I came home from work just after 3.30, and he had written me a note (much as he has before) saying how he can't face his future with any conviction, and he's let us all down (family, friends, church.) A little footnote said he has set off for Beachy Head at lunchtime. I'm so sorry - kicking myself for believing him this morning when he said he was ok! He hadn't slept at all well. I did speak to him around 10.30 from work, and tried to persuade him to make a doctor's appointment. I suspect then that he was already thinking of going. The police have been notified, and I've

spoken to the people at Beachy Head Chaplaincy, (a 'Churches Together' scheme in Eastbourne. They patrol the cliff top 24/7.) I don't know what else to do except wait by the phone and ask you all to pray!
Lots of love Rachel"

Re-reading this, my heart aches for Rachel as she finds the note, rings the police and the Chaplaincy at Eastbourne, and then has to let us all know this awful news. A few days before this she has asked us all to pray for Hugo's release from this dreadful darkness he's beginning to sink into after all the wonderfully creative years he's had since the last *blip* in 2008.

On the fourth page of "*A Creative Journey',"* I get some small insight into his apparently terrifying attacks of clinical depression. Let me quote from him:

"All the great religions teach that there can be no resurrection without some form of crucifixion, no rising without dying, and no life without death. This crucifixion is not some form of punishment we have to endure to pay for our past faults, or the price to be

paid for a better Life, for this is a gift. It is however, what St Paul refers to as the birth pangs of the Christian journey as we grow towards freedom and fruitfulness. As Christ said 'Unless a grain of wheat falls into the ground and dies it cannot multiply.' Any actor has to learn a similar death if they are to create a real character from within during an intensive rehearsal period, rather than merely projecting a theatrical cliché. As one great theatre director said to his cast "You must learn to murder your darlings."

In life this crucifying can mean different things for different individuals, some more dramatic than others, but for me it meant a long struggle with periodic bouts of clinical depression throughout my thirties and forties as I came up against the seemingly insurmountable barriers along the path of my creative and spiritual journey. This is the heart of the story I have to tell in Act Two of this memoir. The climax of this play for me was when I lay huddled at the edge of Beachy Head on the Sussex coast on the coldest day of the year, trying to summon the courage to jump. However as my mother and father were fond of saying The Show Must Go On! So rather than landing in a crumpled heap some hundreds of feet below, I felt now as if I had been miraculously reborn."

During this walk through the valley of the shadow of death in 2008, he agrees to a spell in the small psychiatric ward of the local hospital, submitting to various therapies. I speak to him each evening and I know he longs for the day when he is discharged. Every day he is visited either by his minister from their wonderfully supportive church, or by some of their many friends in the congregation or from his colleagues in the Drama department at Hurtwood House, the sixth form college where he teaches. His father, who at that time has a small flat in London, is also able to make the journey. They persuade me not to travel from the Midlands, as he already has Rachel and so many local friends visiting each day. Instead I make do with that precious daily phone conversation with him. Sometimes mothers do have to take a back seat!

After that time he has another long period of creativity, both working with his drama students at Hurtwood as well as at The Space. Apart from his writing, he is also presenting many shows, directing some superb productions, including a memorable "A Midsummer Night's Dream", and a poignant production of Thornton Wilder's "Our Town". My youngest granddaughter, Katy, has a small part – her first but not her last I'm sure. Her sister Charlotte is on the sound desk, and of course Rachel is, as always, in the cast. Hugo and Rachel work together as a creative team. He as a wordsmith and Rachel, with her invaluable musical training and talents, is there providing the musical back ground whenever the production calls for it. A perfect pairing.

January 2011. As soon as 'Hugo Missing' appears on my email, I am immediately in touch with my original home church in Notting Hill, as well as my current local church family, all my past colleagues and friends at The King's Lodge and many, many other Christian friends who know us and love

Hugo. I plead urgently for immediate prayer. We pray to save him from the dreadful death his note to Rachel suggests. Amanda and grandson Joshua move themselves here to stay with me. We huddle together as before, so many years ago, over Adam's murder, finding comfort and perhaps protection, in our closeness. Tim, our church minister, and a couple of other close friends practically move in with us, bringing home-made soups, and feeding us while we all pray. Constant prayer is being offered up for Hugo's life by so very many. This continues for two days and nights. I keep thinking of those cases we hear about, where folk wait for weeks and months, and sometimes even years, to find out what has happened to someone they love. I wonder how they live for so long in this dreadful abyss, before giving up all hope, or breaking down completely. My whole body is taut, stretched to the uttermost, aching with the tension of waiting for news. On Thursday the ringing of the phone suddenly breaks the silence. Holding it in my hand, I listen to the heartbreaking sobbing of Rachel:

"Oh Beth, I'm so sorry, I'm so sorry, I'm so sorry".

"Rachel, tell me what's happened?" Of course I know.

"They've found his body!!" He has slipped past the Chaplaincy team. This time he is determined. This time he is not to going to sit "*huddled on the edge of the cliff trying to pluck up the courage to jump"*. This time he succeeds. All our desperate prayers are not answered....

'And we know that in all things God works for the good of those who love Him' My first knee-jerk response to this well-known Biblical text from Romans is "*really?"* Even as a believer this is hard to accept. How must it be for so many of our non-Christian friends? When my dear ex-husband phones, all he can say is: "*It's unbelievable darling, both our boys?"* His voice is a thin whisper. Yes, we have lost *both* our sons; Amanda has lost *both* her brothers, and they are *both* such violent deaths. Adam murdered, stabbed to the heart. Hugo chooses a crazy hurtling leap of hundreds of feet to his death.

Playing the grieving mother of Judas Iscariot in that powerful American play, I remember the first lines: "*No parent should have to bury a child...No mother should have to bury a son. Mothers are not meant to bury sons. It is not in the natural order of things.*" It is such powerful writing. Further on she says, "*I remember the morning my son was born as if it was yesterday. I was infused with a love beyond all measure and understanding.*" I know I speak for all mothers, even the selfish ones like me who plan to get back onto the stage, or whatever their careers may be: that moment the baby is placed in our arms after all the struggle of birthing is a moment that is ineffable. Probably I remember my daughter Amanda most. She is our first, and she is 'his princess.' But each birth, each baby is the most precious moment in every mother's life. The thought of their death is inconceivable.

Rachel is amazing. She sets about organising all the practical necessities, and is even brave enough to be driven down to Beachy Head, and find the exact spot from which the Chaplaincy team presumes Hugo leapt. She also has to deal with getting the death certificate and the possibility of dealing with a Coroner's court in the near future. Instead of collapsing in a heap and metaphorically asking for *the smelling salts,* she rises gloriously to this tragic occasion. Their church family is constantly close beside her and the two girls. Again I see the support and love we receive from God's family. Daily phone calls are coming to and fro between us, making sure we are all coping. In Horsham, Rachel is arranging all the details for Hugo's Thanksgiving Service at the large Parish Church, a fortnight hence. It seems as if all this activity and her determination to make Hugo's service the most beautiful she can create, is her way of showing her enormous love for him. I'm hardly consulted. It reminds me of their wedding. It is *their* wedding, not mine! Now I am only too glad to leave it in her hands. She and Hugo planned so many memorable events together. On her own now, she is doing this for him. It's going to be unforgettable. And it is....

I look through the handsomely printed six-page Order of Service that Rachel has been so busily arranging. Her musical training at the Royal College of Music, and growing up in a family where music is so central, shines throughout the service. Three days later, I send a group email to as many friends as I can think of. As that memory is so immediate, let me quote some passages from it:

"There are one or two of you – my dearest friends, that I haven't been in touch with yet, and I'm sure as the days go on I will realise so many more I need to tell. Hugo's life came to an end on the 20th January, having ended it himself while in one of those deep dark places that stalked him every three or four years. I am probably at the very lowest ebb in my life since the last heartbreak with the murder of our dearest firstborn son Adam, just twenty three years ago. Now the loss of Hugo just before his fiftieth birthday this year is something I could

never have contemplated. I have to remember it is not only my heart that is breaking, but that of his beautiful sister Amanda, who has now lost both her brothers, and is feeling lost and alone. I hardly recognised his father's face yesterday at the service; like me he feels broken. Rachel, wife to Hugo and mother to his two lovely girls, has been an incredible witness, a tower of strength putting together a glorious "THANKSGIVING SERVICE FOR HUGO'S LIFE" at Horsham's beautiful thirteenth Century Parish Church which holds just under seven hundred... Over six hundred and seventy, plus all the musicians from the Christians Musicians Network and choral singers fill that space. Amanda's reading of Psalm 139 is spoken about constantly after the service as 'anointed'. The college where Hugo has taught drama for the last twenty years is closed for the day, and the students are sent over in the school bus. It is a highly emotional hour and a half... Hugo and Rachel's church in Broadbridge Heath then served quantities of food and drinks for all the people who can stay after the service. Rachel has received over two hundred cards, and a wonderful book from Hurtwood House, with tributes of love from all the school staff and students.

When I returned to my flat last night, there were more cards and letters, some from people that I have to rack my brain to remember, until I suddenly come across sentences reminding me that: 'My son had been one of Hugo's students, and it was more than teaching him the craft of acting. He had a particular empathy with fatherless lads, and was an important support to him at this vulnerable age.' This is said again and again in the students' tributes. It is obvious how many of their young lives he has touched and inspired, and talked to them about a God that very few of them had ever thought about.

God has given me three children, each of whom any mother would be proud, but presently I feel bereft. This is in spite of so much love I am given from all of you. Forgive me for feeling so dejected. I do love you all, *and will be around again soon."*

For a long time I curl up like a caterpillar in its chrysalis or cocoon. Frances, my chaplain from the hospital encourages me to give myself some time off. Friends send me prophetic words about Metamorphosis, so I decide, having read all these wise words that this is something I can instantly relate to. *"It enters the cocoon as a caterpillar but exits a butterfly. It is a brand new creature when the process is complete. Everything about it is different."*

I read everything I can find about the process of metamorphosis. First and foremost it is a natural transition that takes place in nature, and it cannot be hurried. If the cocoon is broken open before the process is complete, the butterfly will die. It is compared with all birth. There have to be those months in the darkness of the womb to grow the small fetus into that full-time creature it is intended to be. I feel very content to allow myself the unusual freedom of incubating. *"When the process is complete you are going to be absolutely amazed when you see the end product. There will be new perspectives, new strength, new ease, new realms of freedom and new opportunities. Trust Jesus who is the author and finisher of your faith. He has you in His grip, and will not let go. It is all good and the end result will be amazing if you trust Him."*

I am encouraged to write it all out of my system, *"Just write, Beth."* But I find I have no desire to continue writing about how God has changed my life so gloriously. I don't know how to affirm how God can, once again allow such pain, especially in my eighties. It seems unjust. However when it comes to answering questions from friends concerning my faith I am adamant. I write:

"GOING IN FAITH DOES NOT NECESSARILY MEAN GOING WITH SERENITY OR WITHOUT DOUBTS. FAITH CAN BE DIFFICULT!"

Very soon after my Hugo's body has been discovered, despite the constant prayer from so many friends and church groups, I have a phone call asking me if this death hasn't taken my faith away. I cannot live without my faith – so like Peter I have to say: 'where can I go without You Lord?'

I've just been re-reading a book I've had for ages, focusing on a chapter entitled, 'The Experience of Suffering.' I'd like to share a few sentences I find encouraging: "The start of a race is enjoyable. It is easy. Finishing is hard work." I think this can apply to so many of us. You may know what it is to walk in darkness. Sometimes faith _is_ walking in darkness and simply refusing to quit. Sometimes faith is just hanging on. The character of the faith that allows us to be transformed by suffering and darkness is not doubt-free certainty; rather it is tenacious obedience." The author then refers to Abraham's dreadful testing with his beloved son Isaac. 'The road to Moriah can be very dark; much too dark to see more than a few feet ahead.' I can really relate to that. That's why I'm taking life a day at a time for now.

Rachel's next decision is concerning the Memorial Service at St Peter's in Notting Hill.

We have such happy memories of St Peter's where we all started our journey. It's our home church, where Hugo and Rachel married. She is intent on having the service there a couple of months later on the 2nd May. The event promises to be even more glorious than in Horsham! The invitations indicate that it will be two hours long, finishing at 4.00 pm in time for tea and cakes. There is a postscript at the bottom saying: *If you would like to take part in a scratch choir to sing "Zadok the Priest" as part of the service, then please arrive in good time to rehearse at 1 pm.* And finally: *Dress will be smart but not sombre.* Rachel is in her element, arranging another wonderful presentation to Hugo's memory. This time the Ellis family is to be included. We set about getting our talks organised, and Rachel has another beautiful Order of Service sent off to the printers.

Amanda, Joshua and I travel a day earlier to stay with Jean and Graham Ross-Russell in their tall town house in Ladbroke Square. I am able to give Jean a hand along with all the other church ladies, getting all the decorations in St Peter's ready. She is also hosting a party at home for all the helpers, and for those who have travelled from far and wide. Rachel, Charlotte and Katy are all able to stay with us at Jean's on the following day. We're all together again.

My heart gives a double beat as we walk into the church, and hear those glorious, elemental harmonies of "Zadok the Priest," resounding through our beautiful St Peter's. The scratch choir has multiplied. It's the perfect beginning to this extraordinary tribute to Hugo. Looking through the programme, I see that Rachel has gathered over thirty professional musicians to support her. They are to play "Fantasia on a theme of Thomas Tallis" later in the service. The theme of the whole afternoon is based on Ecclesiastes 3, verses 1 - 8: 'A Time for Everything:' - 'A time to be born and a time to die.' Each speaker has a different season to speak about. Amanda has 'A Time to be Born' – about their childhood. I am at the end, 'A time to Die'. Again we have a full church, and it is nearer

5.00 pm at the conclusion. This is the time we are supposed to meet the verger over at St John's garden where Hugo's ashes are to be buried, next to his brother's. People are naturally trying to talk to us, and we are also trying hard to respond to them all but knowing we have to escape, and trying to do so graciously.

I always want to giggle when I look back at that farcical ending of Hugo's glorious memorial service in Notting Hill. I am trying to get everyone moving. Bruce Collins is in a panic because no one has told him he is officiating at the interment of the ashes. Rachel is still happily chatting to a crowd surrounding her, and none of us knows where Hugo's ashes are. Finally we discover them in the boot of Rachel's car, which is fortunately parked right outside the church. We all bolt across to St John's in a most un-Anglican way, madly waving goodbye to all our friends in passing. There's a moment of horror when I discover I've left the money for the verger in my bag that's still over at St Peter's. While Rachel and the girls and Rev

Bruce Collins are waiting to begin the service of Interment, a small huddle of Ellises is standing on the pavement trying to scrape up the £25 that I have left behind. Thankfully Jimmy's son has a £20 pound note in his wallet, and Amanda has a fiver. Jimmy and I have nothing. We rapidly join the others, who have no idea what is delaying us. Bruce just prays a few gentle prayers, while Rachel, as practical as ever, produces Hugo's ashes in a brown paper bag and pours them into the prepared hole. Poor Jimmy is horrified that she has kept them in a brown paper bag, and is furious with me for leaving the verger's fee behind, and I am desolate that I haven't been able to thank all the faithful people who have travelled the one hundred miles from The King's Lodge and Hinckley. However, it is all over yet again! Now we must finally try to settle down. Try to make sense of it. Put all those comforting cards and letters and emails away. Now we must try to begin again....

EPILOGUE

I sit here with the casement window open wide to the sunshine and my small terrace, with its inviting garden chairs. Green lawns stretch to the fence where white flowers of cow-parsley stand high in the meadow. Fields beyond unfold to the distant gentle rise of hills on the horizon. Sheep with their lambs move past slowly grazing, until a sudden four-legged hop from a lamb, called to come to its mother, livens the peace of this pastoral scene. I remember some lines from Rupert Brooke's "Grantchester," a poem I learned and loved at school when I was around fourteen.

"Oh is there Beauty yet to find, and Certainty, and Quiet Kind
Deep meadows yet to forget the lies and truths and pain"

Memories of Hugo fill my beautiful 'given' country home so far from the life I thought I could never relinquish in Notting Hill and enjoying the lights of the theatre, but it's not finished yet.

I started this story over twenty years ago, having very little idea who God was, and where the journey was going to lead me, but now I know one thing for certain. It is only with the intervention and encouragement of everyone that God has sneakily slipped into my path at every bend and crossroad along the way, that I've arrived here in my eighty-seventh year knowing that His ways and truths are fundamentally 'The Choice' I chose to explore in 1988.

And:

"Sometimes Faith is walking in Darkness and simply Refusing to quit."